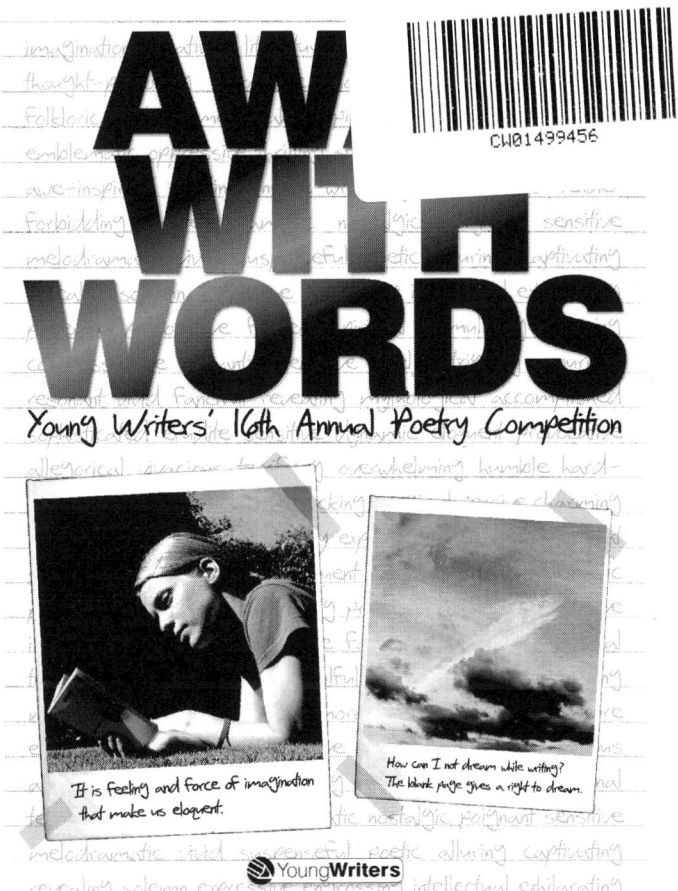

AWAY WITH WORDS

Young Writers' 16th Annual Poetry Competition

It is feeling and force of imagination that make us eloquent.

How can I not dream while writing?
The blank page gives a right to dream.

YoungWriters

Poems From Eastern England
Edited by Donna Samworth

First published in Great Britain in 2007 by:
Young Writers
Remus House
Coltsfoot Drive
Peterborough
PE2 9JX
Telephone: 01733 890066
Website: www.youngwriters.co.uk

SB ISBN 978-1 84431 187 3

Foreword

This year, the Young Writers' *Away With Words* competition proudly presents a showcase of the best poetic talent selected from thousands of up-and-coming writers nationwide.

Young Writers was established in 1991 to promote the reading and writing of poetry within schools and to the young of today. Our books nurture and inspire confidence in the ability of young writers and provide a snapshot of poems written in schools and at home by budding poets of the future.

The thought, effort, imagination and hard work put into each poem impressed us all and the task of selecting poems was a difficult but nevertheless enjoyable experience.

We hope you are as pleased as we are with the final selection and that you and your family continue to be entertained with *Away With Words Poems From Eastern England* for many years to come.

Contents

Francesca Spurdin (12)   35
Kerri Golding (11)   36
Kirsty Moore (11)   37
Caitlyn Cooke (12)   38
Laura Lawrence (11)   39
Laura Ready (12)   40

Havelock School, Grimsby
Linzi Thompson (11)   41
Joshua Orr (12)   42
Robert Margraves (11)   43
Katie Whelpton (12)   44
Alex-Marie Hudson (12)   45
Bethany Stevens (11)   46
Samantha Smith (12)   47
Celine Ward (11)   48
Angela Summersell (12)   49

Kesteven & Grantham Girls' School, Grantham
Holly Porter (12)   50
Shannon Rogers (11)   51
Omolola Salam (14)   52
Anna Fisher (12)   53
Rhiannon Cole (13)   54
Roisin Huskinson (12)   55

Langley Senior School, Loddon
AnnaMae DeJean (12)   56

Lincoln Minster School, Lincoln
Alice Trout (12)   57
Rebecca Mundy (11)   58
Lauren Towell (12)   59
Lucinda Parkes (11)   60
Georgina Seel (11)   61
Leah Palin (12)   62
Alice Jones (11)   63

North Kesteven School, Lincoln
Kyle Mason (14)   64

Queen Elizabeth's Grammar School, Horncastle

Connor Ingamells (14)	65
Alice Jeffery (13)	66
Victoria Marshall (13)	67
Rebecca Martin	68
Neel Radhakrishnan (14)	69
Amy Sharpe (14)	70
Pip Stodgell (13)	71
Jennifer Watts (14)	72
Harry Wells (13)	73
Emma Wyse	74
Leila Alayej (14)	75
Lauren Bark (14)	76
Madhurima Basu (14)	77
Jennifer Buckley (14)	78
Peter Emo (14)	79
Natasha Franklin (14)	80

Royal Hospital School, Ipswich

Bradley Hackett (13)	81
Jessica Hazelton (11)	82
Hester Kenneison (11)	83
Zoë Bull (12)	84
Rosie Motion (13)	85
Jessica Bullen (13)	86
Owen Herbert (14)	87
Alice Blackett (14)	88
Jessica-Leigh Emerson (13)	89
Derek Mackenzie (14)	90
Charlotte Blair (14)	91
Samuel Kester (14)	92
Alice Dryden (13)	93

St Alban's Catholic High School, Ipswich

Anya Bricknell (14)	94
Rachel Carrington (12)	95
Srilekhini Kadari (14)	96
Ben Febvre (12)	98

St Faith's School, Cambridge

Ruth Ilott (11)	100

Emily Whitelock (11)	101
Thomas South (11)	102
Ben Heron (12)	103
Alexander Goyder (12)	104
Robin Harvey (11)	105
Nico Melesi (12)	106
Hugo Phillips (12)	107
Duncan Mackie (11)	108
Larkin Sayre (12)	109
Eleanor Dawson (11)	110
Sam Holmes-Smith (11)	111
James Harrison (12)	112
Ben Griggs (12)	113
Josh Hunter-Jordan (12)	114
James O'Brien (12)	115
Frederick Wienand (11)	116
Chris Anson (11)	117

St Francis Special School, Lincoln

Leah Rumens (18)	118

St Guthlac's High School, Crowland

Tanya Hanford (14)	119
Shelby Sparks (14)	120
Alex Shears (14)	121
Richard Clayton (13)	122
Scott Campbell (13)	123
Ella-Louise Kemp (13)	124
Chelsea Bean (14)	125
George Lersch (14)	126
Hannah Reynolds (13)	127
Sheridan Lambert (14)	128
Aron Sopp (13)	129
Aimee Hobbs (14)	130
Liam Talbot (13)	131
Amy Breen (14)	132
Tony Cole (12)	133
Lucy Hunt (13)	134
Matthew Venni (12)	135
Nicholas Fletcher	136
Amanda Hobbs (12)	137

The Poems

Great White Shark

The silent hunter of the deep
Invincible, no enemies
Except for Man
Hunts with amazing speed
Takes its prey by surprise
The warrior of the ocean
Locked in battle with humans
With teeth as sharp as knives
Master of the sea
Victor of the battle
No one is a match for this beast
With strength that can destroy a boat
But it has a gentle side
Its grey silvery skin
Shining in the cool blue water
Alone and harming no one
But people hunt its flesh
Which makes it fight back
Can't we just leave it alone?
Then it will leave us alone.

Jack Hampshire (12)

Chipped Acrylic

I caught
you
in the
tapestry barn
but she
denied it
even though
I have you
on camera

You charm
smothered
her burgundy
lipstick
and soon
she was
tepid
under your
spell

Her eyes
glazed
like
something
illegal
had wounded
her
innocent
thoughts

You told me
to forget her
she wasn't half a
chipped acrylic
compared to
me

And her lips
didn't fit
perfectly
like mine
on you

But listen to me,
darling
I will say this
only once

I was vulnerable
and I fell for you
'cause you
nibbled
my hip
and stroked
my hair

I will forgive you now
But don't you *dare*
hurt me

I don't forget
And I've been
hurt
before.

Isobel Gordon (15)

Wilderness

I have a hyena in me with my idiotic jokes and my foolish games . . .
It has my rude attitude and it likes to take . . . what it wants it takes . . .
The wilderness gave me the hyena.

I have a mare in me . . . wild as the wind . . .
And reckless as the sea . . .
It has my daring eyes and my wandering feet . . .
The wilderness gave her to me.

I have a dog in me . . . loyal and outgoing . . .
It stands by and protects . . .
It sits quietly by your side and it likes to make you smile . . .
The wilderness gave me the dog for your benefit.

I have an elephant in me . . . she's optimistic and caring . . .
The matriarch of the herd, the one who walks and listens . . .
The one who looks after the people who surround her . . .
The wilderness gave me the elephant.

I have a sloth in me . . . it's slow and negative and always
                                        looking downwards . . .
He climbs from tree to tree unnoticed and unwanted . . .
Clawing its way through the undergrowth . . .
The wilderness gave me the sloth because we all need one.

I have an eagle in me . . . he's brave and stands tall . . .
He flies over the great craggy rocks that are mountains . . .
He hunts with great strength . . .
With wings of gold he soars over land and oceans deep . . .
The wilderness gave me the eagle.

I have a mule in me . . . stubborn and wanting . . .
The mule cares only for food and rest . . .
I need the mule to get me what I want . . .
The wilderness gave me the mule.

I have a tigress in me . . . she's a warrior, a queen of battle . . .
Creeping through the long grass . . .
The wilderness gave me the tigress for my protection.

Georgia Record (12)

It's Just Love

Love, love, love
What is this *crazy* stuff?
Is it a movie?
Is it a person?
Is it a poem?
Is it a colour?
Or is it a feeling?
It's that feeling inside, isn't it?
No one else can feel it for you,
Only you and no one else.
Only you know when it's happening,
No one else.
Just you.
You get those butterflies,
You go all soppy,
But only you can feel it,
No one else can feel it for you,
Only you and no one else
You go all shy,
You blush when you hear his voice,
But only you can feel it
No one else can feel it for you
Only you and no one else
So I guess love is a feeling
It's just . . .
Love, love, and well . . . love
In black and white
It's just love
And it's in the air.

Shakira Cosier (13)
Amberfield School, Ipswich

I Need Inspiration

I need inspiration
It's hard to find at times
When you're searching through the corners of your mind.
I need inspiration.
Can you tell what's right from wrong?
Inspiration could be anything . . .
I need inspiration
Crossing out and putting lines through the words you put when you
were trying to find inspiration.
I need inspiration
What is it? Something you hear?
Something you see
Or something you feel?
I need inspiration.
When you have inspiration you feel like you could keep on
going forever.
No blocks,
No difficulties,
Just an ever-flowing river of words.
Not necessarily about love or hate or death.
Just anything that takes your fancy.
I think I found my inspiration.

Florence Irvine (13)
Amberfield School, Ipswich

Dreams

What are dreams? I wonder at night
It could be something, it could be nothing, it could be anything.
Maybe a castle, planet, or even a cave
It could be something, it could be nothing, it could be anything.
Dreaming of love, peace, whatever we desire
It could be something, it could be nothing, it could be anything.
Thinking of happiness, anger, sorrow and joy
It could be something, it could be nothing, it could be anything.
Maybe a monster or beast to liven things up
It could be something, it could be nothing, it could be anything.
But what of those nightmares? I tremble with fear
That's not something, or nothing, or anything whatsoever.
Nightmares make you quiver and shake
Not something, not nothing, not anything.
Dreams are strange things that can make you afraid.
Which is not something, not nothing, not anything at all.
What conquers a dream? I think in my mind
It can be something, it can be nothing, it can be anything.
Then in a twinkling of my eye I realise how to win the struggle
It can be something, it can be nothing, it can be anything.
Murmuring, grumbling and snoring I awaken from my slumber
It can be something, it can be nothing, it can be anything.
My eyes see the daylight and the dream is now gone
It can be something, it can be nothing, it can be anything.
Departed, vanished, defeated and overcome by myself
It can be something, it can be nothing, it can be anything.
Done with, no more existence, forever lost
It can be something, it can be nothing, it can be anything.
Until tonight when the dreams come back once again
A dream is something, a dream is nothing but a dream is anything.

Madison Smith (13)
Amberfield School, Ipswich

The Terror Of 9/11

I've always found it hard to believe
That something like this could happen,
But then someone told me,
Everything happens for a reason,
Whether it's good or bad,
There's always a reason,
You may not know it,
You may not believe it,
But it happened for a reason.
No one will ever forget what happened,
The terror of 9/11,
When the planes hit the Twin Towers,
When millions of people died in just one day,
When millions of families lost their loved ones,
When the day came that shook the Earth,
The one day that changed the world,
The day that killed so many,
In such a small amount of time,
No one will ever forget,
The terror of 9/11,
If everything happens for a reason
Why did this happen?
What is the truth about 9/11?

Hannah Meara (13)
Amberfield School, Ipswich

Disaster

Only thirteen years since,
I was entered into the world,
But still, five disasters since,
The Iraq war,
Hurricane Katrina,
London bombs,
Tsunami,
Twin Towers,
Shook the world,
Shocked into silence.

I'm finding it hard to believe you're in Heaven,
I can't wait to meet you again,
To see your smile,
To hear your laugh,
To smell your smell,
To speak from my heart,
To touch your skin,
To feel your love.

Francesca Ingram (13)
Amberfield School, Ipswich

Match Point

I feel sick
Here it is
The moment I have given so much up for
The sleepovers and parties replaced by training sessions
The junk food replaced by fruit
I can't breathe
My heart is pounding so loud I'm sure my opponent can hear it
I face the back and I calm myself
Deep breaths in and out, in and out
Then I pick up the perfect ball
I bounce it up and down, up and down
I throw the ball up to serve
An awful toss, I catch the ball
My arm is shaking so much
I can't do this, I can't serve this
Calm down! Don't panic!
You can do this
Bounce, bounce
I throw the ball in the air
I swing my racket, it hits the ball
It flies over the net and straight past my opponent
I scream with delight and throw my hands in the air
My heart is still pounding but this time with delight
With tears in my eyes I look at my parents
This is the best day of my life.

Maddison Jones (13)
Amberfield School, Ipswich

Mother Nature

For every illness
All diseases
There is a cure
Somewhere
Somehow
There will be a cure
There must be
There has to be
Is there?
What if there isn't?
What if the illnesses outweigh the cures?
What will become of us?
What will become of me?
Is there
A cure for cancer?
Somewhere
In the forest of rain
Mother Nature will put the world right
She will prevail
But will it be too late?

Charlotte James (13)
Amberfield School, Ipswich

Gone?

I sat in bed and   w
           o
           n
           d
           e
           r
           e
           d,
               what would happen when I die?

All those memories
           Gone?

Good times, bad times, confusing times,
           Gone?

K	F	H	L
n	r	a	a
o	u	p	n
w	s	p	g
l	t	i	u
e	r	n	a
d	a	e	g
g	t	s	e
e	i	s	
	o		
	n		

Gone?
Are you born again
Or
      Are
         You
            Just
               Dead
                  And
                     Gone?

Amy Hasler (12)
Amberfield School, Ipswich

Why?

I am me, no one else, just me
So when I am me why don't they like me?
So I changed . . . they still don't like me
Yeah I wear black nail varnish
You don't
So what?
I have no problem with the way you wear you hair or make-up
You *still* hate me
Scarred by the words
Hated.
You don't like me?
I died my hair,
Changed my name,
You still hate me
My emotions lost
In my pool of tears
Scars on my arms, grey eyes
Black hair
Screwed up life
My heart's gone, there's just an empty space
No family
No friends
No expressions
I'm a different person, you still hate me
So . . .
I get the rope
It's round my neck
Now I jump
I'm dead
You love me.

Lily Perkins (12)
Amberfield School, Ipswich

Weird Wonderful World Of Questions

What made the ground?
What made the sky?
What made you?
What made me?

Once you've seen the entire world
Does your mind question who or what made it?

Who made the massive whales?
Who made tiny ants?

Was it a bang of light?
Or was it a god?
No one knows why we're here.
Not even great scientists know.
We're just left here to wonder.
We're just left here to ponder.

So many questions with no answers.
Why do we have them?

Philippa Lee **(12)**
Amberfield School, Ipswich

Phoenixes

Phoenixes are fire, are smoke, are free,
They soar and they can cut right through a cloud.
They never die,
But when they do it's not for long.
When they die fire surrounds them, then - *boom!*
Gently ash falls to the ground.
A little sound, a cheep, a cry,
The ash stirs and a yellow beak becomes clear.
The phoenix is back
In five minutes flat!
Phoenixes never die.
Phoenixes are fire, are smoke, are free.

Alice Robinson (12)
Amberfield School, Ipswich

Not Being Able To Be Me!

I miss being able to be me, to have the joys of running free,
They didn't just take my life they took my childhood too.
They invaded our country and took my friends,
And made us wear stars on our clothes.
And then all too suddenly they took us too.
To a place where the walls are surrounded by wire
And your only means of escape is death.
Where you are separated from the ones you love,
And told that you need a shower but see no one return.
Your bed is made for you and seven other people,
And a pair of shoes that pinch.
Where you are to wear thin striped pyjamas,
And to be counted twice a day.
I grew up all too soon,
And learnt about the real world and how it is.
I am alone, and no one knows the pain of not being able to be me.

Daisy Huxtable (12)
Amberfield School, Ipswich

Only Children

We're only children, we don't know a thing.
We don't know about poverty or killings, where do I begin.
In our minds we can see a world filled with catastrophe.
We don't know about divorce or the holocaust.
Little children looking out of the window, trying to figure out why,
Why their dad did it, why did he commit suicide.
We know more than you think, we can reverse everything, 'cause we
are the future of your civilisation, you should hold and cherish us
                                        not push us away.

We can turn it around,
We can put right everything you got wrong!

Hannah Smurthwaite (12)
Amberfield School, Ipswich

Goodbye Emily

Over the years we became one.
We played together, that was fun.
But now it's time for you to go away
I'll think about you every day.
I'm here for you, I hope you know.
It doesn't matter where you go.
I'll write to you, send you things
I'll sit by the phone and when it rings,
I'll hope to God that it's you,
Otherwise I won't know what to do.
You can't just leave Hannah, Alice and me
Otherwise it won't be for us four, just us three
You don't understand I need you
Or I just get left out by the other two.
You would help with that, you were always there
When you were here, I didn't get left out, life was fair.
I will see you then, but not now.
How I'm coping, I don't know how
I know one thing, I have tears
But they will be happy in just three years.

Lily Baxter **(12)**
Amberfield School, Ipswich

Rain Or Pain?

Her lashes were webbed with drops of dew
As her heart beat faster he would not leave her side
He ran his fingers through her hair, but it was willowed
And softly the leaves fell into his hands like stars
Mellifluous, with a capital M, like a child in a game *stuck in smiley faces*
She pushed her head up and desired for wings
She was wild, lost in seclusion
The blistery willow war was haunting, her stomach rolling round
Like an inebriate fool
She clasped her hands together to squeeze the transparent drops,
From the weeping willow tree above her, that had shed his tears
Onto her. Like a snow globe, she was getting shaken up,
Ready to tumble to the ground, but lost in the mist
Her make-up was now smudged, surging down her pale face,
Making her look swollen . . . but was she?
You could not see inside, although her heart was pumping,
As raucous as a child when they are about to open their presents,
Early in the morning on their birthday
Jumping up and down on the patchwork quilt
Yes she remembered, but now she was just like the quilt,
All jumbled up, mixed into the colours
She froze, like a record turning around and around
And just steadily . . . stopping
Like her, yes her, whoever she was the record . . . tranquil . . .
Or corrupted in time
But she had to be someone, or she wouldn't be feeling that teardrop
Or raindrop . . . but was it pure or beastly?
Was it rain or pain?

Scarlett Saunders (12)
Amberfield School, Ipswich

Questions

What is the meaning of life?
Is it for love
Or is it for freedom?
Is it for happiness
Or is it for hate?
Maybe ambitions
Or even to care?
Whatever you think
The question is there.
Why?
Why is the question
We ask every day
Why did I do this?
Why did I do that?
Why is this here?
Why is that there?
Why can't I be?
Why did I do that?
Why didn't I do that?
Why am I happy?
Why am I sad?
Why is the question
We ask every day.

Molly Clyne (11)
Amberfield School, Ipswich

What Am I?

Look at me
Am I gold or
Am I silver?

Why do I feel
I don't exist
No more, not ever?

Blue and green
Or pink
Am I man or even sea?

Bumpy and blue in the face
But maybe not or maybe,

Hurt inside
With numbers through my throat,

Cut my mouth
Falling with loads of blood

Then I realise
Who I am
Not you

But me.

Hannah Wilson (11)
Amberfield School, Ipswich

I'm Not Ill - This Is My Life

Hunched by the wall.
I sit.
Staring into infinity.
Not seeing.
But knowing what's there.
It's all covered.
It needs to stay clean.
'Live.
Cleanse.
Breathe.'
I mutter those words silently.
I focus on a wall.
It doesn't matter which.
The words are all written,
There, copied endlessly.
Wherever you look.
I'm surrounded.
I scream.
Suffocation closes in.
But it's reassuring.
Becoming enveloped in the words.
I stare.
They fuse together.
Blurred.
I let out another scream
Strangled.
They have to be clear.
Clean.
I can't live if they're
Dirty.

Amelia Quine (11)
Amberfield School, Ipswich

Irony Of Existence

Your voice is not my motivation
My discontinuation is not your stimulation.
Aspirations and ambitions.
Guarded by his inhibitions.
Those eyes he seals me with.
Drain my soul of life and living.
Mine is just another loveless, lifeless cry of desire.
A desperation plea.
Primarily I have to flee.
Razor blades and sheets of glass.
He hurts me so why can't I?
The irony of our existence is creeping shallowly behind.
Soon you shall be just another picture for me to burn
An added grievance to my dignified reality that is life.

Olivia Wilkerson (15)
Amberfield School, Ipswich

When Will She Know?

Innocently, she sits across the room from me. Smiling and laughing
as if she is on top of the world.
But then the thought goes through my head.
Does she really know what's happening?
How I know something that's going to change the life of my friend
sitting opposite me.
Is it fair she has no idea of what's going on? Isn't it her right to know?
That day by day when she moves on so quickly she doesn't realise
soon it'll all be gone.
Yet the person she's going to lose doesn't even know herself.
Both totally oblivious to the fact that something's slightly wrong.
She hasn't got long to realise, soon it'll be too late.
Her whole world will fall on her, an unbearable fall, nothing compared
to what's happened before.
A fifteen-year-old girl.
An innocent girl, with an innocent soul, who just hasn't seen
any of the signs.
The other, her friend, guilty of knowing something too hard
to keep inside.
The secret her friend holds contains her life.
Everything that keeps this girl together.
The only thing she can depend on, care about, is slowly losing grip
and she doesn't even know.
Yet when are they going to tell her?
Life isn't fair. She doesn't want to know, she doesn't want to keep
this life-changing thing from her friend, but would it hurt her more
if she knew?
Two close people spending every day with each other.
One with an innocent soul. One with a guilty soul. Close friends.
Trying to act the same around her, when really she can't -
she knows too much.
Can she keep this from her friend any longer? Soon it'll all come out.
Her friend asks her what's wrong.
'Nothing,' she replies. But it isn't nothing.
How can it be nothing when it's a terrible event about to happen
in just a few weeks, and no one knows.
Except the one girl who doesn't want to know.

She can't go on like this, she just can't.
It's too hard for her to handle.
She panics, but doesn't want to let anything out.
But no one knows.

Except the girl who doesn't want to know.

Sophie Maitland (15)
Amberfield School, Ipswich

Broken Silence

The winter winds blow softly through the trees.
All is still and silent,
The snow falls gently to the ground.
Each flake, a little dancer, gently spinning through the sky,
No noise it makes, no sound at all,
There is silence, resting peacefully in the air.

In the spring the birds are singing,
Their chirpy voices fill the air.
The warm fresh breeze winds through the budding daffodils,
In the distance the church bells ring,
Calling people to its doors.

The summer loud and bubbly,
Waves come crashing against the golden sand,
The warm air is filled with screams of happiness.
Screeching are the seagulls as they swoop above our heads,
The footprints on the sand lay still and untouched.

The autumn winds are blowing,
Screeching and screaming through the sky,
Tearing the crisp brown leaves from their homes on the branches.
A deer gallops softly across the fields, moist and brown,
Its hooves gently crunching the leaves beneath its feet.

Again a new year comes around,
But no silence is there now,
No birds are singing and no snow falls to the ground.
Just the roaring of an engine,
A car goes whizzing by.
You never see a rabbit or a bird up in the sky.
There is no more field for the deer to run across,
But in its place a hard black road,
Filled with lorries, cars and a bus.

Lucy Homer (15)
Amberfield School, Ipswich

Courage To Survive

Brutally beaten,
Starved
Tortuous, unpredictable games
Not a son but a slave
No longer a boy but an it
Despair
Deprivation
Every day I feel this pain.
I'm just a little boy, dreaming of a family to love me and call me
                                                          their son.
The outside world knows nothing of the nightmare played out
                                              behind closed doors.

Childhood memories I will never get back
Worthless
Ugly
Fat
Stupid
So pathetic
Disappointment
Robbed of my life - determined to survive.
To find a dream and make something of myself
A destroyed life in a cruel world.
But at the end of the day I still love her and must have the courage
                                              to survive!

Amber Rainford (14)
Amberfield School, Ipswich

Armageddon

On the corner of Buckwell's corridor, between the towering presences
of M&S and Starbucks,
Is the home of George McCree,
Fifteen years ago he gave up his high-powered job, his friends,
his family and went to live on the streets,
Dressed in scratchy clothes, moving with lice and infection,
Shoes; worn but hardly conceal toes black with cold,
A cigarette drips from between his chapped lips
Labouring breaths chug snail-trails of smoke onto the street,
Snapping eyelids, glancing into faces of strangers,
Between his fingers is a sign,
'The end is nigh' it states
Inked on with ancient board marker; hardly readable
He stands on the cobblestones, his back to his sleeping back
and stock of cans,
Pleading his case,
Fifteen years ago he gave up his high-powered job, his friends,
his family and went to live on the streets,
He has never looked back since,
A HSBC account holds his virtual money,
And a shaggy Beagle (laying by his feet) is his companion,
George McCree is the sign we have all been waiting for,
Sometimes people stop in the street when they see him.
Others walk on past, oblivious to the miracle,
A man is pounding the pavement, his briefcase grazing his thigh.
He sees George from a distance and his eyes go wide,
When he reaches him he stops and stares . . . he has seen the sign,
He slowly puts his briefcase on the ground,
George hands him the sign, picks up the briefcase, and walks on
Fifteen years ago Adam Johnson gave up his high-powered job,
his friends, his family and went to live on the streets,
He has never looked back since.

Charlotte Jones (14)
Amberfield School, Ipswich

One

One more death, one more family,
One more city, one more country.
One more person, killed by famine
Killed by illness, killed by war.
One more death, one more family,
One more city, one more country.
What's the difference?
What's the problem?
It isn't us who need to care
It isn't us who need to share
One more death, one more family,
One more city, one more country.
But we are rich,
And we can help
We have life
And we have wealth
We have jobs
And we have schools
We have choice
So do we have duty?
One small change can make a difference
One decision, change the world.
One less death, one less family,
One less city, one less country.

Rebecca Hasler (14)
Amberfield School, Ipswich

Through The Eyes Of A Death Knight

As it stalks the barren wastes it created,
Holding up its sword, serrated,
Crushing the skulls of the already dead,
Dreams of its death running through its head.

The blur of its steed's bones in the night,
Summoned forth by unspeakable rites,
Bones of the netherworld are blending,
Into the blackness it appears to be bending,

Lightning flashes, shield appears,
Spikes protruding like phantom ears,
Bearing the blood of unknown legions,
All lives were taken, without reasons.

To battle it rides, to kill once more,
Powered by a demonic lore,
Crying for the blood of a thousand men
Rushing quickly, into their den.

It rides forth, onto the steep hill,
Staring through eyes, red as the kill,
And laughs its laugh, that could shatter plaster,
'That's another land for my master . . .'

Dale Robinson (14)
Arthur Mellows Village College, Peterborough

The Phoenix

Its wings are spread wide
Its majestical wings glow
It dives to its side
Far from slow

Its beauty is pure
Its feathers aflame
Defies you to think
Any two are the same

She soars in the sky
High above the clouds
Flying so high
Above the massed crowds

Its eyes appear sad
For this phoenix mourns
Its sibling was killed,
But its soul will live on

For the phoenix once slain,
Leaves a new life in its ashes
But that is never the same
As the one that is gone

But this phoenix moves on
For where else can it turn?
Its home is now gone
So it will never return

The phoenix looks forward
To its future ahead
Never looks backward
Yet continues instead

This phoenix true - is pure at heart
So here it goes to make a fresh start.

Duncan Young (14)
Arthur Mellows Village College, Peterborough

Handheld Love

(For my Nintendo DS)

O shiny image of my heart's desire
You doth tempt me daily with your great love
Your thoughtful challenges I doth aspire
At constant peace with you my turtle dove
No visual screen hath shown thee better
I longingly yearn to reach the end
Your vibrant text a passionate letter
My pulsating sad heart forever rend

I haltingly speak to thee as if real
You respond a tempting blue fading screen
And to complete thee is the final deal
A shockingly shimmering shameless sheen
You, the ultimate game, I beat thee yet
You are an ageless friend, a toy, a pet.

Jamie Giggs (15)
Arthur Mellows Village College, Peterborough

What Am I?

I can be long and thin like a tree trunk
Or small and squished like a tin can
When alight I burn so bright
I can also dribble down the side like raindrops
But be careful I can be dangerous
And I can give a soothing sensation slowly through a room
What am I?

Rebecca Stephen (12)
Attleborough High School, Attleborough

What Am I?

I am like a block of white cheese
I'm as creamy as a biscuit
I spin like a never-ending washing machine

You can see me but I'm a million miles away
You can see my face staring straight back at you.

I'm brighter than a light bulb
I bring light when it's dark
I smell and taste like gorgonzola

I am as round as a football

What am I?

Evie Joannou (12)
Attleborough High School, Attleborough

What Am I?

My switch you can turn,
To make me bright like the sun.
I am hot, I will burn.
I will jump when I'm hit.

I am round like a ball
Sitting silently watching,
Crash! I could fall,
When no one is there.

I am your sun in the sky,
To brighten your life,
To help you see,
To help you be,
In the light!

Francesca Spurdin (12)
Attleborough High School, Attleborough

What Am I?

I'm as high as the sky,
You can't reach me,
I'm round and crescent too,
At day it's hard to see me,
At night I play peekaboo.

I look at the world in a way,
That when I shine you see,
The face of the man inside me,
Like snow on a tree.

What am I?

Kerri Golding (11)
Attleborough High School, Attleborough

What Are They?

They screech like a baby's high-pitched cry,
They bang when they hit the sky,
Then they light up like the Northern Lights.

They use fire, so please watch out, the flame is very wild.

They hurt people when they act silly,
Or they scare animals until they shake,
But are loved when they're used right.

Boom! Bash! Bang!
They go off,
'Til late at night.

Do you know what they are?

Kirsty Moore (11)
Attleborough High School, Attleborough

What Am I?

I am taller than the clouds,
More mighty than the Queen,
Stronger than an ox,
What am I?

I am an upside-down ice cream cone,
And as pointy as a giant pair of scissors.
I slice the sky as the wind blows past me,
What am I?

Caitlyn Cooke (12)
Attleborough High School, Attleborough

What Am I?

I have mostly a rough texture,
But still I can be smooth.
I am brown like a delicate hazelnut,
Very dull and I wouldn't say I'm glossy
But I do stand out in areas.

I am like a person standing
As I stand up tall inviting the warmth of the sun,
And making sure it is welcomed.

Most of the time I am not alone
But joined by other types,
I don't have bones
But I have various homes
And can live almost anywhere.

I live for many years, you would be surprised.
I wave my arms when snow settles on me
Because I get a frosty feeling and feel the cold.
I like living in peaceful and pleasant places,
I am a habitat for many wonderful creatures,
I grow sweet, succulent flowers and juicy ripe fruits.

Laura Lawrence (11)
Attleborough High School, Attleborough

What Am I?

I am as colourful as the moon!
I am as bright as the sun!
I am as light as light as a lemon!
There are millions of me!
I am out all day!
But I can only be seen at night!
I silently stay standing through the night!
But curl away in the day!
I always stay alight!

What am I?

Laura Ready (12)
Attleborough High School, Attleborough

I Put A Sign On My Door

I put a sign on my door,
But not one like before,
It says *Do Not Enter,*
In big fancy letters,
And also a picture of doom,

But if you ignore the sign,
And decide to go inside,
You will meet certain death,
Just for the best,
And you won't come out alive,

But if you somehow survive,
Then you will find something I have tried to hide,
My small book of secrets,
For those who shall seek it,
Glued to the bottom of my chair,

I put a sign on my door,
But please try to ignore,
The cravings to peek inside,
Although you will probably be eaten alive,
Do *not* enter my room!

Linzi Thompson (11)
Havelock School, Grimsby

The World

The
World
Is a football
Teaming with life
Floating through space
Without a care in itself
Circling round its heat source the sun
Horror, terror, love and friendship
Common feelings on its skin
Our home
Revolving round
His child is near as
His brothers are years apart.

Joshua Orr (12)
Havelock School, Grimsby

Field Of Fire

They're covered in the lush green grass
Like a carpet soft and red,
Then came a wind, it blew down the poppies
Like a scythe through a field of straw.
Up they stood so tall and stood there
Like a solider all around the season.
A season later down comes the snow,
It covers the flowers like a carpet cold and white.
Here comes the spring, the snow has melted
But no sign of poppies anywhere.
Up came the sun so great and hot
Burning, burning, burning a lot,
Up comes a head
It rises like the sun, the head soars.
They covered the lush green grass
Like a carpet soft and red.

Robert Margraves (11)
Havelock School, Grimsby

Losing My Best Friend

(In memory of Hailey from South Parade - she left me on my own, she died)

I'm losin' my best friend,
But they've been gone for months,
Tried to pretend things were the same, but they're not
Want things to go back to the way they were,
But we've changed, neither of us is the same person that we
were before.
Don't know what I'll do 'cause she's gone for good
All I ever wanted was to be understood,
Losin' my best friend. The one person I thought I could trust
A best friend is someone you can turn to,
Ring at any time of the night,
Someone to understand why you've gotten in a fight,
Who you trust more than anyone else,
Someone who may not share your opinions but trusts your intellect.
Someone who will be there when no one else is
Losin' my best friend,
Well I've lost my best friend,
But I guess that's okay,
'Cause my mum had too many doubts to trust in them anyway.
Well this isn't a hateful song,
It's full of good thoughts about a friend that left me,
But those good thoughts kinda slipped along the way,
And now I'm just left with nothing but these words
And an empty space where,
My best friend used to be . . .
Losin' my best friend,
Yeah, my best friend that left me.

Katie Whelpton (12)
Havelock School, Grimsby

The Jungle

Orange-black with stripes,
Prowls the jungle at midnight
Sees the birds like coloured stars
Soaring through the sky,
Like a savage's dart
Hear the giraffe munch on trees.
Watch the elephant drink from the seas.
See the leopard and cheetah run.
The life of the jungle has just begun.

Alex-Marie Hudson (12)
Havelock School, Grimsby

Winter Poem

Winter is an old man,
Gloomy and frightening,
He huffs and puffs at you,
As you step on his lawn of beautiful white grass.

He pinches you with his cold, clammy hands,
On your cheeks and on your ears,
He shoots bullets of whiteness flying your way,
So make sure you wear your protective gear.

He pushes out the moon,
Until we are in darkness,
And covers up the sun so the days are dead,
We are in gloom and tiredness.

Young sporty sun versus the old evil man,
Sun pushes the winter out of the way,
The only remains of the long winter months,
Are the slowly melting snowflakes, transforming in the sun.

Bethany Stevens (11)
Havelock School, Grimsby

The Classroom

Drip, drip
The rain went
Everybody at work
Doing their poems
Discussing ideas
Then a slam of the door as it closed
And then it opened again and
In came the head teacher,
So angry, so red
She roared and she stamped
As everybody looked up
So scared and frail
She shouted, she screamed
And then she walked out
And we all got back to work.

Samantha Smith (12)
Havelock School, Grimsby

Storm!

She sits in the room watching the telly,
Her knees trembling a bit like jelly,
Then out of the blue, some lightning appears,
Lighting up the room,
Then a *roar* of thunder, and a *big boom!*
Like flickers of fire being hit at the roof,
The girl hides in fear of the sound,
She seems to know what's coming with a bound,
Then with a *thud!*
And with a *thump!*
Then *crash,* the rain starts to pour down,
The girl looks out of the window in despair,
Not daring to go anywhere near,
She looks at the sky,
It looks like a giant waterfall creating,
And washing everything away,
The rain sounds like bullets being hit at the door,
Then clattering onto the floor,
Then with a *thud!*
And with a *thump!*
There is silence all around.

Celine Ward (11)
Havelock School, Grimsby

A Field Of Poppies

Poppies, poppies everywhere,
Like little love hearts on a chair
Poppies, poppies everywhere
In the fields and in my hair.

I stand and look at the fields of red,
The colour is lovely in my head,
A big red sea for me to enjoy,
With all the other girls and boys.

But when they're picked the field goes green
And we have to remember what we have seen,
And wait until another year,
When the lovely red poppies will again appear.

Angela Summersell (12)
Havelock School, Grimsby

The Place

There's a mouse,
Who owns a house,
That gets scared,
When he sees a woodlouse.

The house is scary
And it's owned by Mary,
Mary's scary,
She only eats dairy.

The house is on a hill
With a mouldy window sill,
It's never been cleaned,
But it overlooks a mill.

It overlooks a park,
Which is made of bark,
It's very dark,
It's very dark.

Holly Porter (12)
Kesteven & Grantham Girls' School, Grantham

Those Chavs

Those chavs they wear the hoodies
Those chavs they steal the goodies
Those chavs they do the smokin'
It's them who'll end up chokin'

Those chavs they think they rule
Those chavs they think they're cool
Those chavs don't at all rule
They're the ones who play the fool

Those chavs they drink the booze
Those chavs they always lose
Those chavs they do the crime
It's them who always look like slime

Those chavs get themselves into trouble
Those chavs increase themselves by double
Those chavs they think they rock the house
It's them who'll end up pleading sorry like a mouse

Those chavs they skive off school
Those chavs watch TV then drool
Those chavs they do speakin' funny
It's always them who take our money.

Shannon Rogers (11)
Kesteven & Grantham Girls' School, Grantham

Girl Never Learns

Like a moth to the flame
You made the same mistake,
Like a serpent luring his prey
He promised you the world,
What you got was his poison,
Killing you slowly but surely.

And now you scream,
You swear that you're dying.
Your crimson tears,
A lasting mark of your pain.
Now you've crashed and burned,
You pick the ashes of your life.

Like a warrior's spear,
Hurt pierces your heart.
Like your worst nightmare,
The memories of him don't fade.
They haunt you day by day,
Threatening your very sanity.

And then you find your so-called hope,
All of the pain seems to disappear.
He promises you the world,
You gladly believe him.
Who wouldn't with those eyes?
Like a moth to the flame.

Omolola Salam (14)
Kesteven & Grantham Girls' School, Grantham

Toothbrush

I am bristly
I get used twice a day.
I am like a Hoover
But I get drowned in water
And smeared in toothpaste.

I go around in circles
And sometimes get dizzy.
I come in different shapes and sizes.
When you go on holiday I always come with you,
And when I am old I get thrown away
With not a care in the world.

Anna Fisher (12)
Kesteven & Grantham Girls' School, Grantham

At The End Of The Bed

There I sit at the end of the bed,
Watching the world happen around me.
I started off bigger than my owner,
But as she has grown her feelings for me have diminished.
I have been sick on and cried on,
Tears of happiness and sadness,
Spun around in the washing machine,
Then hung by my toes on the washing line.
My fur is matted and my pink dress is stained.
I have been passed down through the family,
But she did care for me the most.
I have been from Devon to Spain,
From camping to a five star hotel.
But now she is 16
I am just another item.
All of my friends have been and gone,
But I have stayed here waiting at the end of the bed.

Rhiannon Cole (13)
Kesteven & Grantham Girls' School, Grantham

The Tower

These waters I think I know,
Whose secrets will they show?
A baby's, a child's, a peer's?
Not mine though.

The fish must think it queer,
For the water to end right here,
Just before the wavering tower,
So far away, yet so very near.

A kick and a splash made with great power,
Reaches an inland flower,
Not another sound is made,
'Til a breeze reaches the tower.

The waters are a lovely shade,
Swirling out over the glade,
Where a castle is ready-made,
Waiting for another age,
Waiting for another age.

Roisin Huskinson (12)
Kesteven & Grantham Girls' School, Grantham

The Path Of Life

Oh how life is a path of risks and chances
Which makes us stronger and physically enhances us,
We fight through life winning and losing
We fight through life healing and bruising.

The award of success and the materials of wealth,
The chance of living long by having good health,
Life is a roller coaster, go anywhere you please,
Closing and opening doors whilst finding new keys.

Having the pleasure of meeting new people,
Some may be nasty, some may be feeble.
Having good friends for the rest of your life,
Falling in love and becoming a wife.

Settling down with some kids and a dog
Rolling in mud and playing with frogs,
Going for walks and watching the scenes
Getting a good job and buying a 40 inch screen.

Watching yourself growing old and getting grey hair,
Not wearing any age products because you don't really care!
Spoiling your grandchildren, seeing them smile,
Making your long life all worthwhile.

Finally you're gone as quick as that,
To start a new life and make it from scratch.
No memory of anything or anyone,
So now you're a baby sucking your thumb.

AnnaMae DeJean (12)
Langley Senior School, Loddon

The Disappointing Wake Up

Pink-faced.
You are really sensitive, lovable and do not fear making friends.
Courageous.
Strong willed.
Learning that life never runs smoothly.
Roses are what make you tingle.
What are you trying to find out?
Why do you worry so much?
Why are you worried about being yourself?
'There is something that is pulling me down, I can't tell.'
I know something is wrong, I know it.
I like you.
But I have got to find you.
You only exist in my dream.

Alice Trout (12)
Lincoln Minster School, Lincoln

My Heroine

Long blonde, curly hair, swaying as she walks.
The only middle-aged woman with the power of ice.
She moves like an elegant angel.
You groovy person!
Eyes as blue as the sea.
Her skin as soft as a linen blanket.
Why are you so beautiful?
Your father is a successful god.
Why are you so brave?
Lucia Hope.
Strange Town thinks you're a hero!
But . . .
I know you are my friend.

Rebecca Mundy (11)
Lincoln Minster School, Lincoln

My Heroine

Blonde hair, swirling in the wind.
The only teenager with the power of Earth.
Flying like a bird.
You cool thing.
Eyes full of determination.
Skin soft like a baby's skin.
Are you brave?
Why are you pretty?
Your grandma has power of water.
Emily Smith.
Pleasntview thinks you're a hero!
But . . .
I know Nikki is the sister of an evil prince.
Hello.

Lauren Towell (12)
Lincoln Minster School, Lincoln

Leona

Sweet teenager,
Unlike most teenagers these days.
Moves like an angel floating in the sky.
You look happy and joyful.
Flitter, flitter, flitter, I can hear you come.
Leona.
You smell like the summer breeze.
You love unicorns.
Are you a unicorn?
People think you're crazy that you think unicorns are real,
But,
I know they are.

Lucinda Parkes (11)
Lincoln Minster School, Lincoln

Who Are You?

Delicate pink face walking gracefully like an angel from Heaven.
All you like is to be kind to people and to look out for them.
Moving like Heaven, gentle and soft.
Eyes looking curiously into the amazing night-blue sky.
Your skin feels smooth like a feather fallen from a bird.
You're as brave as a shield being hit at full pelt by a sword.
You can't hear your soft feet touch the hard floor.
You smell like fresh roses just being picked.
The world thinks you are beautiful.
You look so happy with your great big smile and delicate face.
Your family love you for who you are and no one else!

Georgina Seel (11)
Lincoln Minster School, Lincoln

Searching For Life In A Stone Heart

Brave and heroic stands the statue of Melony Harper.
She looks down
At all the wondering people gazing into her hard stone eyes.
How people wonder
Who she is, what she is doing here, why she is here.
She is a mystery,
Almost a dream.
Her past shall never fade away,
Her past is a memory and a memory it will stay . . .

Leah Palin (12)
Lincoln Minster School, Lincoln

The Poem Of Tremendous Happiness

Amazement whirled around the room as she entered.
Longing to be able to touch her and know her.
Imagine the surprised faces as she tells everyone!
Tremendous applause is given.
Her eyes study her father, his face cold.
'I'm ever so happy for you both!'
A perfect way to end the perfect story between two silly dwarf men
                                        and the man of her dreams!

Alice Jones (11)
Lincoln Minster School, Lincoln

Changing Face

Now I feel like everything is changing,
except the names and faces.
Feel like I'm engaging,
something that travels at faster paces,
than myself.

And now the people I found important,
have disintegrated into nothing.
Changed, I feel like everything isn't quite buoyant,
and nothing works anymore not even screaming,
because I know it won't change a thing.

And maybe one day I'll find a person,
that takes me away with words,
but I'm unsure, dwindling and uncertain,
staring at everyone, seeing cowards,
but realising I'm staring in the mirror.

Removing all the images of the people I call friends,
and staring at one with tears in my eyes.
The one of smiling face, everything gels and blends,
and there's me staring hopelessly into the skies.
Nothing can end this,

except you, the one that,
without a doubt,
takes me,
away,
with,
words.

Kyle Mason (14)
North Kesteven School, Lincoln

Again

(Inspired by Shakespeare's 'Romeo & Juliet)

'Twas a warm summer's eve,
I was sitting in the east,
As Dominic, my sun, was preparing to rise,
Again.
Arise fair Dominic, my sun.
And kill my envious heart once more.
In front of this dark jealous moon.

Parting is such a sweet sorrow.
As the day transformed
Into the night, my Dominic disappeared.
Again.

I shall say goodnight
Until you rise.
Again.

Connor Ingamells (14)
Queen Elizabeth's Grammar School, Horncastle

Bleak

(Inspired by Shakespeare's 'Romeo & Juliet')

As you look out of the window all you see is bleak
And that parting, that parting of souls left you bleak
And you wonder, and you wonder if this is all love has to offer -
Bleakness
And as you look out of the window at the dull sky, the cold turns
to the thing you fear most
Bleakness, such bleakness

The last thing you felt, you remember feeling
Was sweet, all embracing passion
Which turned to the violent pain of sorrow
But now it's just bleak

Until one moment when you stopped feeling
Was when you said goodbye
Goodbye to happiness
Goodbye to hurt
And now you're left bleak

Until you embrace happiness
Until you embrace sorrow
And until you understand happiness
And until you understand sorrow
You'll be trapped in the prison of bleakness

So leave the window
Leave the bleakness there too
Break free from the prison of bleakness
Embrace your feelings.

Alice Jeffery (13)
Queen Elizabeth's Grammar School, Horncastle

The Beginning Of The End

(Inspired by Shakespeare's 'Romeo & Juliet')

It is the beginning, the beginning of the end.

The sun may rise in the east,
But it sets in the west,
It always sets, always goes away,
Like love.
It suddenly appears,
It's not very bright,
But it gets brighter and brighter,
Higher and higher,
Then it starts to fall.
Down, down,
Until it disappears,
Leaving the cold night sky,
Lit only by the blank disc of the moon,
I plead,
Arise, fair sun and kill thy envious moon,
Destroy all envy, hatred and evil,
But it never does.
Love never stays for long,
Parting with it is such sweet sorrow,
It will come again,
I shall say goodnight,
Till it be morrow.

Victoria Marshall (13)
Queen Elizabeth's Grammar School, Horncastle

Untitled

(Inspired by Shakespeare's 'Romeo & Juliet')

It was in a room that could fit no more guests
That the two lovers first locked eyes.
Juliet was in the east of the room, and Romeo in the west.
In that room so dimly lit, the sun shone down as they realised.

From when that love did arise they were happy and in love,
The fair sun seemed to forever shine.
But Romeo did not know how much he meant it,
When he said: 'I'd kill for our love, yours and mine.'

The couple were together but nobody knew
And when an envious man became aware,
A moon fast replaced the sun.
So Romeo felt he had no choice, but to give this man a parting
from earth and air.

The end is such a sweet sorrow because,
One day Juliet said, 'I shall say goodnight.'
But she never said, 'Till it be morrow.'
And together they died with love as their only right.

Rebecca Martin
Queen Elizabeth's Grammar School, Horncastle

It Is A Tragedy

(Inspired by Shakespeare's 'Romeo & Juliet')

It is a tragedy, 'true love';
In the east
When a new day begins,
And Juliet thinks it will not die,
It is inevitable that
The sun will set,
And the day will soon end.

Arise fair Juliet, it is a dream,
It will not last; and like the sun,
And like life itself it will die
Or perhaps be killed,
By the envious thoughts,
Whilst you, are over the moon.

You might think parting is unbearable,
But such a fool you are;
Love at first sight, what a sweet thought,
But one that can only be followed by sorrow

That feeling you think is love,
Is nothing more than lust;
I do not think you shall be happy,
Despite you saying you will,
Good advice is to end it now
Just as night ends day,
Till the time you know more,
It would be wise to slow down;
Or else in the morrow,
You will find yourself, lonely and disowned.

Neel Radhakrishnan (14)
Queen Elizabeth's Grammar School, Horncastle

Envisaging Envy

(Inspired by Shakespeare's 'Romeo & Juliet')

It is dawn again.
My dreams of you ruptured
By the rooster's crow.
Alas I gaze into the east
Ivy twisting onto my balcony
And you Romeo, my love
Walking down below.
My presence unrecognized
As your fair hair dances in the sun
Arise my heart awoken.
Roaring, an imprisoned lion
Needing to break free
Mine rib cage entrapping it, held hostage.
It cries all tis not fair.
The sun rises rapidly with elegance
Dreams are killed, yet still live on
My body envious of my mind
Like the moon now envies this fine sunny morn.

Amy Sharpe (14)
Queen Elizabeth's Grammar School, Horncastle

Fading Love

(Inspired by Shakespeare's 'Romeo & Juliet')

It is cold. I am cold. The light is gone.
Hijacked by the east, they say. And I am not alone.
He is here. Marco is here. With me.

The light went not long ago, when the sun disappeared in the mist.
It should rise, like the dead, but the fair sun won't appear again.
Not for me. Not for us.

And yet I am comforted, though the night has killed before.
The love between us . . . not passionate, but envious.
And I loathe him for it.

The moon won't shine; I asked it to.
Parting with such sweet light is unbearable.
Such a shame it's my entire fault.

Sweet smells are wafting, delicate roses flowering,
But all I feel is sorrow. And that is how it kills.
I shall be going now, alone again, for he has said goodbye.

The sun will not be gone for long, for he has finally left.
Again.
He is the dark.

Loneliness overpowers me, the night killing again.
Not killing till the time is right, or it will get no pleasure.
I will be gone tomorrow, for he has killed again.

He killed me.

He killed my love.

Pip Stodgell (13)
Queen Elizabeth's Grammar School, Horncastle

Universal Romance

(Inspired by Shakespeare's 'Romeo & Juliet')

It is the east, and you are the sun.
We set our paths about you.
Never daring to pass you by.
We cannot, will not leave your side.
Wishing to feel your warmth,
To see your beauty
Until the very end of time.
You are blessed with such blinding beauty,
And yet your dazzling beams must give us the gift of sight.

From the first day, we set forth to stay in your glory always,
For we are devoted and dependent,
Desiring your natural radiance,
Yearning for only your warmth. So
Arise again, fair sun, and again,
For when you are set we are half plunged into darkness,
But for the taint of an envious moon.

And though we worship only you,
Sometimes, on occasion, we do hear a blue moon whisper silently
Behind us that which we fear most.
But it cannot, will not happen!
And though we daren't turn, the taunting behind us is understood.
And though parting is such sweet sorrow,
We know we must turn to the gloom for now
And say goodnight until tomorrow.

Jennifer Watts (14)
Queen Elizabeth's Grammar School, Horncastle

Shrouded Beauty

(Inspired by Shakespeare's 'Romeo & Juliet')

It is the darkness, enshrouding
The beauty, which holds its grace.
From north, south, east or west,
And anywhere else, her face,
Is the, becomes the, dark sun.

Will arise from that darkness
But with a certain air,
Betraying the mystery,
With a face, so wild but fair.

The darkness, can be broken only by sun
And only at its brightest, will it kill
This shroud; fuelled by the love of one,
But will return under glare of the envious moon.
And lay still.

But the touch of mine will send this cloak parting
It is such, that I may call it sweet sorrow
And that I, with my heart (which shall be smarting)
I will say, good! Let this night cloak fly,
Till it would be morrow!

Harry Wells (13)
Queen Elizabeth's Grammar School, Horncastle

No Tomorrow

(Inspired by Shakespeare's 'Romeo & Juliet')

The feeling of love
Falls rapidly when left heartbroken.
It is the east,
And he wishes he was the sun.
My dear, the sun has gone,
And it will kill the envious moon.

Parting with you has left me
Alone.
It is such a sweet sorrow.
That when I say goodnight,
To that old love of my life,
I guess there will be no tomorrow.

Emma Wyse
Queen Elizabeth's Grammar School, Horncastle

Not So Romeo

(Inspired by Shakespeare's 'Romeo & Juliet')

It is the east, and *(insert name here)* is the sun.
Arise, fair sun, and kill the envious moon . . .

The morning after the night before,
Parting is such sweet sorrow, that
I shall slip away, not stopping to say
Good morning.

The night is hazy in my mind
I walk till it is clear and
Hate to be alone but I won't be on my own,
As soon as it is morrow.

Leila Alayej (14)
Queen Elizabeth's Grammar School, Horncastle

No Anything

(Inspired by Shakespeare's 'Romeo & Juliet')

Parting with my love,
Is like parting with my heart.
Such pain is always caused,
As we are torn apart.

Sweet moonlight lights my way,
Through the deep and darkened shadows,
Sorrow and damage building inside,
As my heart fades away
Into the goodnight sky.

Morrow, oh morrow the sun come forth
Unto this blessed morn.
A new day with new pray
With my life like a fresh-born fawn.

No more pain for my poor heart to take,
No longer am I at stake.
No grief, no anger, no hatred.
No crying, no worry,
No anything.

Lauren Bark (14)
Queen Elizabeth's Grammar School, Horncastle

Just Like Planets

(Inspired by Shakespeare's 'Romeo & Juliet')

Beauty is the east and we together
Are as powerful and as blinding as the sun.
Together, united, we will arise,
To kill the mocking moon,
The envious moon.
Our families are the moon,
As weak as the moon, envious like the moon.
However, together we are strong as the sun,
And we'll defeat the envious moon.
The earth is our child, interesting and beautiful,
The stars will be our children,
Magnificent and luminous,
They will help us search for happiness through partings
And will give light in the dark times of our lives.
However, for us parting will be a sweet sorrow,
And death sweeter and softer still . . .
Glistening drops of rain will wash away our pains and sorrows.
We will remember joyous times and happy memories together,
After we say 'goodnight' and lay in bed,
And fall into the lands of slumber and dreams,
Forever together, far from planets and the envious moon.
Tomorrow shall approach,
And our love will be reborn.

Madhurima Basu (14)
Queen Elizabeth's Grammar School, Horncastle

Beauty Like The Dawn

(Inspired by Shakespeare's 'Romeo & Juliet')

It is dawn, and the sky in the east
Is as enrapturing as you.
I am reminded of you,
And how beautiful my world became
When you, Ruby, walked into my life.

Your hair glows with radiance,
It is just like the morning sun.
When you arise and we meet
Your fair beauty puts even the sun to shame.

Together we can triumph, and
Kill those who are envious of
Us, leaving them alone like the moon,
Jealous of how fortunate we are
To have each other.

When the day comes to a close,
I cannot bear our parting.
It is such, that I feel I will perish from sweet sorrow.
Then I shall realise I shall see you on the morrow,
I can bring myself to say farewell,
As we shall not long be parted.

And as we part with a joyous
Goodnight I can be at peace,
Deep in my heart I know it
Will only be till tomorrow.
Then once again we will be together,
Lost in our happiness and love.

Jennifer Buckley (14)
Queen Elizabeth's Grammar School, Horncastle

A Light In The Winter

(Inspired by Shakespeare's 'Romeo & Juliet')

It is a long cold winter,
to the east is a shadow,
and to the west is Juliet,
or is it the sun in a dress?

Arise, she will, like the fair sun,
and kill all her envious foes,
as well as destroy the shadow in the distance,
a shadow of the hideous moon.

Parting from her bright home,
it is such a magnificent place,
her sweet face is full of sorrow,
it is such a shame that I shall forget.

As we part I say goodnight,
till the next time it will be lonely,
for Juliet is a one and only,
thinking of her as I wake tomorrow.

Peter Emo (14)
Queen Elizabeth's Grammar School, Horncastle

It Is Ra

(Inspired by Shakespeare's 'Romeo & Juliet')

He sits, stares across the desolate plains,
Gazing into the east,
Distant ants worshipping and pleading,
For here, Ra is the sun.

Ra scorches, hardens the mocking earth,
Burning their sore eyes,
Laughing at hopes of rain, assuring
Famine and toil has begun.

They beg, 'Have pity, do not arise, fair sun.'
Offering plenty and receiving little,
The sun kills all hope.
Their jars lie still and empty.

He watches, envious of the distant cool sea,
Waiting for the cool moon
Parting its glass with such iridescent light,
Drifting his eyes over the scenery.

He wonders, is the night so sweet?
Remembering the sorrow of drought,
The desolate eyes, that the loneliness
Etched lines of toil onto their faces.

He cries, 'I shall say goodbye!' and the
Surrounding night will come,
Feeling so fresh and clear,
Relieving them of the sun's cruel embraces.

Till the sun brightens and flows,
Filling the world with searing light,
It is the beginning of the end,
And it shall be tomorrow.

Natasha Franklin (14)
Queen Elizabeth's Grammar School, Horncastle

Memory

Sight, speech, hearing, touch
But not my memory.
As I walk my final mile,
As I breathe my final breath,
As I say my final words:-
I'll take my battered, happy memories.
Safe in my grave, they'll be forever:-

Undisturbed.
Understood

But all the same,
If after life is abyss,
Or life again;
I'd leave my memories gladly.
For the fact that I lived these memories,
I would forsake them.
Those marks that will fade.

Bradley Hackett (13)
Royal Hospital School, Ipswich

Picture This

This is the picture of my mum, dad and me,
This is the picture that Mum keeps happily,
This is the picture that makes me so sad,
This is the picture of Mum, me and my dad.
This isn't the picture that stayed ever true,
This isn't the picture Mum keeps the years through,
This isn't the picture of a horrible fight,
This isn't, and I wish that this picture was right.
Those lucky people who have parents together,
Are people who will not see this picture ever.
Those people won't have memories of their parents breaking up,
And will have a happy family, I wish them good luck.
Imagine if I didn't have a picture like this,
My parents would be together, what bliss.
But maybe it wouldn't be that good after all,
My sister, brother, stepmum and dad would not know me at all.
Of course I love my family, it's how it has to be,
But still that picture brings memories -
Of my mum, my dad and me.

Jessica Hazelton (11)
Royal Hospital School, Ipswich

Tristram And Iseult On Board Ship

Deep, deep into the night,
A sudden sadness woke him with a fright.
Pacing the deck of the ship he did find,
Iseult standing as if blind.
Standing there to jump from the boat,
She wanted to drown for she could not float.
Tristram carried her down into a cabin,
Together they loved secretly loving,
For all the long night,
Until morning light.
Forever loving,
Secretly caring.

Hester Kenneison (11)
Royal Hospital School, Ipswich

Sporty

Rugby is a game for men,
Who can't read or write or count past ten.
Mud layers from head to toe,
Mum will go mad *no! No! No!*

Hockey is that game for girls,
But not the ones that do a twirl.
Hitting, tackling, pushing, gliding,
Scoring a goal, cheering, sliding.

Tennis is a game for those,
With springs that live between their toes.
15-love, 15-all.
'Come on then, hit the ball!'

Cross-country is a sport for all,
It pays if you are very tall.
Long legs sprinting, jogging, pacing,
At the end of the day it's all about racing.

Rounders is a game for all,
It includes equipment bat and ball.
Running round and round, don't stop!
Let's hope that the ball will be dropped.

Netball is a game for me,
But it's not everyone's cup of tea.
Passing, running, shooting, scoring,
Hear all of the crowd cheering, roaring.

Don't ask me why but football's cool,
I enjoy kicking and heading the ball.
Captain of my under 8s,
Showed me the sport, it was great!

Zoë Bull (12)
Royal Hospital School, Ipswich

My Sister Was Back

I got out of school and ran all the way home
I slammed down my bag and books
And pushed my way into the living room.
I saw her standing there
As real as life
She smiled at me and did a shy wave
I produced a broad grin
And jumped over the sofa
And gave her a big hug.
She hugged me back
And pushed me away
Looked me up and down
My sister was back.

Rosie Motion (13)
Royal Hospital School, Ipswich

My Grandad

When I think of him I shed a tear
Even though it's been over a year
The time has gone for drinking beer
The time has gone for us to cheer
To threaten me with twisting my ear
Or laughing about the ghosts we fear
In the stories we have to hear
Or in the boat that you would steer
Laughing if we got too near
A rock, or you would shout, 'Oh dear.'
If I was frightened you would sneer
As if I thought we wouldn't go clear.

But Grandad I'm sad, it's been over a year
From the days you liked a lot to cheer
The teacher saying it's not what you want to hear
But what you don't want to hear I fear
That's when I let out a big, 'Oh dear.'
I really was sad, it wasn't clear
I didn't think your day was so near
I miss you Grandad, I want you here
I miss you so much, I want you to steer
I even miss you twisting my ear
I wouldn't mind you ever drinking beer
When I think of you I will always shed a tear.

Jessica Bullen (13)
Royal Hospital School, Ipswich

At The Beach

It was a boiling, blistering, baking day at the beach.
There were millions of people fixed on the compacted sand.
The sea was ice-cold but that did not stop anyone from going in
With a boiling hot chocolate in one hand.
It was a quiet day, only the occasional scream rang out.
It was a superb experience as the splendid day came to an end,
Which was a terrible doubt.
The tide was lifting off the rocky beach.
The day had to finish when the rocks were reached.
The smell of sandy wet bodies aroused in the car
And a bitter taste came up in my mouth
As if we had nearly been to Mars.
The sand, the sea, the salt,
All gone . . . gone . . . gone . . . gone.

Owen Herbert (14)
Royal Hospital School, Ipswich

Drunk And Disorderly

He would leave the house,
And not come back till late.
He would be ever so loud,
And scare me when he came back
Slamming the door,
Climbing the stairs.
He had been at the pub.

Mum would lie in bed,
As he shouted at her,
So mad, mad with rage,
He was drunk.
He did it every night,
It was so awful.

My dad, an alcoholic,
I hated him for it.
He had ruined my life
My mum's and mine.
He was scary and violent,
He hit me and kicked my mum.

Alice Blackett (14)
Royal Hospital School, Ipswich

My Dad

I want to see my dad again,
I just don't know where or when.
I think of him every night,
I think he runs from fear and fright.
I want to see my dad once more,
I want to hear his footsteps outside my door.
I look at his picture on my wall,
Just waiting for one little call.
I want to see my dad again,
I just don't know where or when.
I want him to hold me like I was a little girl,
He used to call me his little pearl.
Sitting there in front of the telly,
I used to sit upon his big belly.
I wish for just one moment with my dad,
That moment will never come again.
That just makes me sad.
I read his gravestone every day,
I can remember it like a script from a play.

My dad . . .

Jessica-Leigh Emerson (13)
Royal Hospital School, Ipswich

My School

I really do love my school
Especially when the teachers are made a fool
The only thing that is short is our hair
You can eat in lesson if you dare
Some of the people tread on your heels
Another thing that's great is the meals
We don't watch too much telly
Our rugby team really puts in the welly
Our bed areas are never messy
No one here is ever fussy
We are well-behaved especially at night
It's great no one here has time to fight
OK maybe I said a few lies
Well I am not exactly going to die.

Derek Mackenzie (14)
Royal Hospital School, Ipswich

Untitled

Your eyes twinkle like stars in the sky,
When I hear your words they make me cry,

When you look at me and smile,
I wish to be with you more than just a while,

When you touch me with your hands,
I wish we could run away to a faraway land,

When I dream about running my hands through your hair,
I realise I'm not with you anymore, that is so unfair.

But now I have you for evermore,
Please don't walk away like you did before.

Charlotte Blair (14)
Royal Hospital School, Ipswich

Clouds

It was on a sunny day,
When the clouds wanted to play,
Each one of them had a say,
Of what they wanted to do that day,

One wanted to make Man pay,
By making it a horrible day,
They hovered over the sea bay,
And thought all day of what to play.

Samuel Kester (14)
Royal Hospital School, Ipswich

A Midsummer Night's Dream

(Inspired by Shakespeare's 'A Midsummer Night's Dream')

On her eyelid, it did fall
An enchanted droplet oh so small
A change of true love, oh so cruel
Oberon, a jealous fool.

For the time she came to wake,
The consequence of cupid's mistake,
On her the love curse would fall,
To change her true love once and for all.

Her name Titania, oh so magic,
The love spell oh so tragic,
Her love fell upon an ass
Her love, to be such a farce

Away in Athens tears were falling,
Denied to follow cupid's calling,
Hermia planned to be eloped,
Of this luxury she was choked.

Demetrius had the blessing
For Hermia's wedding
Hermia loved Lysander
Oh, how much love does meander.

And here we had the dance of lovers,
He loves her but she loves others
Rhyming couplets for the lovers
But what about all the others

Hippolyta with freedom to express
Bottom with an asshead dress,
This story, destroying, changing love,
Due to cupid, a mistake from above.

Alice Dryden (13)
Royal Hospital School, Ipswich

Ordering

I've been told to write a poem.
But I really can't be bothered.

It has to rhyme and make sense.
Yet the only thing I write is nonsense.

My fingers twitch to count the syllables
Only I haven't any to count.

Forced writing makes me ill.
But I can't plead physical sickness.

There is a list of subjects on the board.
Yet I don't have inspiration.

Everyone is still writing away.
But only I can write this poem.

I've been told to write a poem.
And I have just finished it.

Anya Bricknell (14)
St Alban's Catholic High School, Ipswich

The Giraffe

Silent, tall and graceful,
The giraffe moves around,
Beautiful yet imprisoned,
For it cannot make a sound.

Tall, thin, elegant,
A lovely mottled pattern,
Beautiful yet imprisoned,
Cut off from communication.

It wanders about now,
Eating trees near to it,
Beautiful yet imprisoned,
As for sound - not even a bit.

What is its name I wonder
How did it come to be here?
Beautiful yet imprisoned,
For it cannot cry a tear.

These questions can't be answered,
These answers cannot be found,
Beautiful yet imprisoned,
Is the giraffe that makes no sound.

Rachel Carrington (12)
St Alban's Catholic High School, Ipswich

If You Stand Beside Me God, I Will Make The Most Of It.

Why cannot I walk?
Running, skipping and falling,
What can I do to keep me alive?

Why cannot I hear
The sounds of laughter and joy?
What can I do to keep me alive?

Why cannot I see
The beautiful scenery and nature?
What can I do to keep me alive?

Why cannot I move?
Oh why cannot I be like everyone?
Please God tell me what to do.

Shall I cry
Or shall I fall to my knees and
Do absolutely nothing?

Waiting for someone,
Someone who can care for me,
Please God help me.

I want to be just,
Like everyone who have all
The things they need

They can see, hear
Walk, move and do everything,
But why is it just me?

Do I have a
Loving family to support me?
To feel affection for me?

I know,
God please stand beside me
And I will make the most of it.

And I will try,
To make the most of it,
Keep me alive just like everyone else.

Srilekhini Kadari (14)
St Alban's Catholic High School, Ipswich

What Are You?

What are you?
You who crawls in the darkness
Who wriggles
Into my ear
Some filthy
Unseen presence
Whispering untruths
You
The black cloud on the horizon
The wolf among
The sheep
Of everyday life
I sense you in the dark
I feel you in malice
I curse you in fear

My friend
Purchased a car
And you gnawed at me
Like a dog at a bone
And I felt
Jealousy
Your hound
Stroking me with a
Mutilated muzzle
You caused me to be snide
Afterwards
I resolved never to
Listen to you
Again
But your barbed teeth
Had snared my soul
I cured your name each
Time
You forced me to speak with
Crude words

Your sour lips
Muttering
Commands
Now I have no friends
You rule my life
And so I ask of you
What are you?

Ben Febvre (12)
St Alban's Catholic High School, Ipswich

Creation

Darkness . . .
First pitch-black, a prison, nothing,
A spit of fire, or light, then
A glowing moon and Heaven's sun is born,
Now silver stars in the midnight sky,
A sudden morning, a pine tree forest,
The soul of a mountain.

A jug of aqua liquid, pouring into a deep crust,
But with fishes of the rainbow
And salt of the crystals,
Finally, the finishing touch . . .
Life . . . life of Man and animal,
For this is no gift . . . this is creation.

Ruth Ilott (11)
St Faith's School, Cambridge

Young Writers - Away With Words Poems From Eastern England

Tiger . . .

A tiger is like a still-life picture,
Waiting to pounce on its startled prey.

Like a bolt of lightning,
So alarming to some but exquisite to others.

Like a shining red ruby,
Perfect in every manner.

Like the ocean,
Unexpected,
Companion or rival.

Like magic,
Miraculous in every way and form, approaching from anywhere.

Like a volcano,
Spewing out with rage,
Telling us it's there.

Like a kaleidoscope,
Getting more appealing after every turn, the centre of attention.

Like a river,
Moving soundless except the leaves rustling in the background,
Flows with a motion.

Like a mouse trap,
Instant kill,
Erratic,
Volatile,
Capricious.

Emily Whitelock (11)
St Faith's School, Cambridge

The Creation

In the silver light of the moon
The last white wolf howled
Its wailing song, yearning
To see another of its kind

It howled its mournful song
All night and all day long
To see another of its kind
In the desolate silver mountains

It was once part of a large herd
It could remember the times when
Its family had played happily together
But then the hunters came
And killed them all

He was alone in the world
Alone, afraid and unhappy
Suddenly a lone figure
Walked towards him

Now he could see it wasn't one
But an entire herd of . . . white wolves
You could feel pure joy radiating as he ran towards the herd
To start a new life in a new place.

Thomas South (11)
St Faith's School, Cambridge

Young Writers - Away With Words Poems From Eastern England

The Creation

A vacuum. Completely blank.
A blaze of glittering green
The slurp of a slippery tongue
Crept out from under a dense, dark canopy
The sense of rough skin
And a dull grey snout appeared from under a rock
The aardvark sneaks up on its prey.

Ben Heron (12)
St Faith's School, Cambridge

Tiger

Death,
A lurking nemesis waiting to kill you in one final attack,
Crouching in the corners until the time is right.
Leaping like a ghost, you don't know what's happening
Until it's too late.

Gymnastic,
Leaping gracefully from place to place,
Powerful sinews, muscles all help to catch the prey

A mouse trap,
Drawing you towards it with a prize,
The speed of the attack is faster than lightning,
Whatever comes near won't be coming back.

Beauty,
Wonderful and graceful, a being of power,
Perfectly symmetrical in every way.
As if a mirror was put in-between his face.

Volcano,
Looking safe but it is unpredictable,
It can explode in a furious wave of power destroying all in its path,
Nothing can stop it, you better get back.

Story,
The stories of a hunter, will he get his prey or will it elude him?
The creeping up then a problem but the problem is always solved.

Magic,
The tiger is magic, it appears out of nowhere,
Like a magician's hat empty, but all of a sudden
The tiger jumps out with his claws aiming for you!

Alexander Goyder (12)
St Faith's School, Cambridge

Red

Red is a subtle colour and with the power of the bright red flame.
And with hope from the red petals on a rose.
And destruction the colour of the flames in a house fire,
And respect in the robe of the king.

Robin Harvey (11)
St Faith's School, Cambridge

I Should Like To . . .

I should like to feel the smooth rhythm of classical music
as it passes through the throat of the gramophone.

I should like to bend down and listen to the soft speech
of the soft green grass.

I should like to be able to read the strange thoughts
of the grandfather clock as the hour passes.

I should like to catch and keep the happiness
of a Christmas morning in a small transparent jar.

I should like to open a door with my mind.

I should hope to find a place where all of this is possible.

Nico Melesi (12)
St Faith's School, Cambridge

Red

Poisoned apple,
Danger sign,
Hazard warning,
Bloody murder,
Fighting anger,
A carnivore,
A spillage of paint,
A blazing inferno,
An erupting volcano,
A baking oven,
A sign of death,
A fire bird,
A devil red,
Satan's pet,
A crime scene,
An angel of death,
A predator's prey,
A bottle of red wine,
A red rose petal,
The sweet smell of crimson,
A holy meaning,
A sign of love,
The sign of completion,
A sign of wickedness,
A heart failing,
Are you red!

Hugo Phillips (12)
St Faith's School, Cambridge

Creation

Imagine . . .
An empty universe, non-existence,
A single bright light,
As a planet begins life,
And sets off on its infinite journey,
Around the solar system,
Alpha, Beta and the other early Greek numbers,
The planet's volcanic core,
Silently bubbles and froths,
Under hundreds of kilometres of solid, near impenetrable rock.
This planet will see many millennia,
But for now,
It is silent, lifeless.

Duncan Mackie (11)
St Faith's School, Cambridge

I Should Like To . . .

I should like to pluck the shimmering stars from a moon-drenched
summer's night,

I should like to taste the gentle morning breeze
and savour it on my tongue,

I should like to capture a lick of flame in my palm
and feel it caress my fingers unharmed,

I should like to effortlessly shift a sky-high mountain
to clear myself the perfect view,

I should like to paint a die showing all six faces at once,

I should like to soothe the proud lion at the zoo pacing
its cage restlessly,

I should like to feel the thrill of a crowd washing over me,
wave after wave of energy and excitement.

Larkin Sayre (12)
St Faith's School, Cambridge

Who Am I?

I am the girl in the picture.
I am the girl who no one knows.
I am the girl in the bridal dress.
I am the girl of the sea.
I am the girl with the long golden hair.
I am the girl, deserted and lonely.
I am the girl in the white frothy waves.
I am the girl by the gravestone.
I am the girl looking into the ocean.
I am the girl of the ghost.
Who am I?

Eleanor Dawson (11)
St Faith's School, Cambridge

White

A pointless sight,
Bizarre look,
Mind twisting,
Endless confusion,
Plain . . . boring,
Unknown purpose,
Holy meaning?
Or
Evil meaning?
The angel's blanket,
A fluffy, silent snowflake,
The snowman's emotions,
Paper's feelings,
Completely pointless,
A cloud of simplicity,
A maze of complexity,
The sign of Christmas re-rising,
And the morning breeze,
A wasted mind, so blank,
A repeating face,
An uninspiring irregular shape,
Its long hidden secrets,
Boring background,
A peace maker,
The white fire night,
And,
An empty heartbeat!

Sam Holmes-Smith (11)
St Faith's School, Cambridge

The Birds Are . . .

The sky is the freedom, the high of highs.
The birds live in freedom, they twirl, they swoop, they fly.
To fly is to live.
We think we are the best, the rulers, we are not, the birds are.
All human souls are bound to a cage of arms and legs,
While our soul longs to fly and experience the wind in the air,
To get from here to there, to pull a few gs and dance in the wind,
A bird, the ultimate existence, all we can get is a metal bird, the dreams,
All humans dream of being a bird.
The falcon.
The seagull.
The eagle.
The albatross.
The greatest of all.
The birds are.

James Harrison (12)
St Faith's School, Cambridge

The Tiger Is King

Tiger is like a king,
The tiger is the emperor of the volatile decreasing jungle,
Directing the way of life and sitting with glorious pride.

Tiger is like a rainforest,
The tiger moves gracefully around the ever-endangered,
Delicate tropical rainforest,
Controlling its ill-fated prey.

Tiger is like a criminal
The tiger can lash out at you anywhere, anytime, any way he wants.
His deadly, spine-chilling nature is capricious.

Tiger is like an athlete.
The tiger and the athlete are agile, nimble and alarmingly supple.
Their sinews twist and turn putting huge amounts of strain on their all
powerful muscles.

Ben Griggs (12)
St Faith's School, Cambridge

Tiger, Tiger

Death, like an ever-hungry storm
waiting to unleash itself on anything
or anyone that dares get in its way.
Flowing through the long grass like a
river in pristine condition.
More elegant than a gymnast, flexing its muscles.
King-like, as if watching over every animal in its kingdom.
Powerful, as powerful and as power-hungry as the strongest warrior.
Beauty, graceful yet unforgiving should anything get too close.
Like lightning striking and then vanishing in a flash
is the tiger.

Josh Hunter-Jordan (12)
St Faith's School, Cambridge

Tiger, Tiger

The tiger pounced resembling a mouse trap
It flew off like a firework so bright and colourful,
A spring pinging,
It's a tiger that kills like a python's venom,
A well dignified hunter,
It has emotion of which angry until dusk,
For the last drop of perfection
It's like a gymnast as it pounces from tree to rock
Its muscles working hard and tiredly,
It's got electricity, it's fast and rapid
It can speed up to fifty mph
It stands with pride like a statue with power and controlling glory.

James O'Brien (12)
St Faith's School, Cambridge

Tiger

Like a river
flowing over the grass in a fluid, elegant
motion stalking his condemned prey.

Like elegance
sleek and streamlined the tiger pads
along softly, gracefully and silently.

Like fearsome beauty
his gleaming striped fur, his fire eyes
shining in the impenetrable darkness of the night.

Like passion
sly as a vixen, he dodges from place to place,
he's there and now he's not.
His mind unfathomed.

Like a drop of perfection
lustrous, muscled, devious and clever.
A perfect killer.

Frederick Wienand (11)
St Faith's School, Cambridge

Tiger, Tiger

The tiger is like a king
It is the pride of the vast, the timeless and almighty jungle.

The tiger is powerful. It's like a powerhouse
Charging a city of light.
A city of light for a god, all in its fiery eyes.

The tiger's claws ready to bring swift death to all its victims who
dare cross its path.
They are a many-edged sword blade ready to charge to battle.

The tiger chases you in a never-ending fashion
A racing car speeding around at a hundred miles an hour
Not stopping for any reason until it is pleased with its bloody feast.

The tiger is a making of pure evil at the hands of Satan.
Made for pure destruction and annihilation.
Even a god could not match its powers.

The tiger's face,
Older than time itself,
Like a flowing river flowing for all eternity.
Never stopping and has never begun.

Chris Anson (11)
St Faith's School, Cambridge

Life Through My Eyes

I have seen death.
I have witnessed life.
I have observed love and watched strife.

I have surveyed helpfulness.
I have scrutinised selfishness.
I have pitied the strong and admired the weak.

Why do the powerful turn cheek
When the vulnerable sit and weep?
Why sow but not reap?

I have gained knowledge from my eyes.
Now nothing can surprise.
I've felt the breeze through my leaves.
You guessed it. I'm a tree.

Now it's your turn to see.
What age can do for thee.

Now just let me be.
Where I relax and see.

Leah Rumens (18)
St Francis Special School, Lincoln

My Teddy

My teddy is very cuddly,
She keeps me warm inside.
Whenever I'm upset,
I've got someone to cuddle,
So whenever I'm out,
And my teddy's on the bed,
I'll be home soon,
To give her a snuggle.

Tanya Hanford (14)
St Guthlac's High School, Crowland

Beautiful Flowers

Flowers are beautiful
They smell so sweet
Shining bright colours
And dull dark ones too.

Flowers need light, water
And rich soil too
Flowers will die with no
Light or water.

Flowers are beautiful
They smell so sweet
Shining bright colours
And dull dark ones too.

Flowers are beautiful!

Shelby Sparks (14)
St Guthlac's High School, Crowland

Young Writers - Away With Words Poems From Eastern England

All Good Things Come To An End

As I lay here I don't stop to think of anything else,
By hurting you I've hurt myself.
It's solely losing you that's on my mind,
Depression overcomes me I soon find.
Maybe I've lost you; maybe you were with me the whole time.
Paranoia is the only reassurance I know.
I continue to think it may be time to grow.
We got on so well, we fitted just perfect,
Although I didn't think you slipping away would hurt me so much,
Are you worth it?
The tears cease to stop even though I know they will dry up.
The pain however will not.

Alex Shears (14)
St Guthlac's High School, Crowland

My Mum

My mum's name is Sarah
She is the fairer.
She tidies the house
But screams when there's a mouse.

At where she works
She is a clerk.
She's got a shiny new ring
She doesn't like to sing.

She is going to get married
A bouquet she will have carried.
Her dress is a secret colour
And that's my mother.

Richard Clayton (13)
St Guthlac's High School, Crowland

Apples

Apples are yummy, apples are sweet
I like to eat apples a couple of times a week.
Some are red, some are green
Some are yellow or in-between.
Others are sweet or even sour
I couldn't eat more than one an hour.

They can be grown in France or
The English countryside
They can be used for juice or cider
Or even Appletizer.

So when you eat an apple remember what they say:
An apple a day keeps the doctor away.

Scott Campbell (13)
St Guthlac's High School, Crowland

I Miss You

I wished upon a shooting star, to see the boy I miss
Oh how I would give anything, for just a simple kiss.
It's hard to be away from you, for more than a few days.
I hope I'm not obsessing, and it's only just a phase.
I hate that I can't talk to you
And rarely expect your call
It weakens me not to hear your voice, and eventually I feel I'll fall.
I miss everything about you, your kiss, your laugh, your smile
I wish that you could come and see me, even if it's only for a while.
I want to just hold your hands, and for you to keep me warm,
I feel so safe wrapped in your arms; protected and safe from harm
All I want is to be by your side, and to still feel that you're mine.
I'm sure things will all blow over, and everything will be fine.

Ella-Louise Kemp (13)
St Guthlac's High School, Crowland

My Sister

You may think my sister is cute, sweet, a pain,
Or just insane.
But you don't know her as well as me
Obviously.
Ever since the day she was born I've loved her
I protected her but now she protects me!
Even though there's 10 years difference we're closer than ever!
Nothing will ever change that, never!

Me and my sister Becker enjoy our company
She puts make-up on which I must admit don't look the best on me!
We play in the back garden
We talk a lot of jargon
But she means the world to me.

Chelsea Bean (14)
St Guthlac's High School, Crowland

The Only One

The way she talks,
The way she walks
Long blonde, smooth hair,
She doesn't have any cares.

The lasting memory in my mind,
She is so sweet, tender and kind,
I love her,
But there is no return.

Talking to her makes me feel,
That I could love and heal,
When I'm lying in bed at night,
Memories of her, firmly in my mind.

George Lersch (14)
St Guthlac's High School, Crowland

Best Friends

B uddies for life
E nemies never
S tay
T ogether

F orever
R eliable
I n groups
E nergetic
N o rubbish
D ependent
S trong for ever.

Hannah Reynolds (13)
St Guthlac's High School, Crowland

Giant's Delight

Vats of soup
On table trays
Side of shark
With mayonnaise
Haunch of ox
With piles of mice
Mounds of gristle
Served on ice
Bone of mammoth
Head of boar
Whales and serpents
By the score
Tons of coleslaw
Stacks of rabbits
(Giants have such
Piggy habits)
Then, at last,
There comes a stew
Full of buffalo
And ewe
Followed by
Some chocolate cakes
Big enough
For stomach aches.

Sheridan Lambert (14)
St Guthlac's High School, Crowland

Why I Don't Like My English Teacher!

She always sets loads of homework for when we get home,
Like making up poems instead of talking on the phone.
Sometimes she says we have to do a booklet
On preparation for the SATs.
At the end of the day we won't have time to feed the cat.
Really she is a good teacher,
But she should give us less to do,
This is why I don't like my English teacher,
Now I'm asking, do you?
So, when all is said and done
My homework's here to see.
I hope I get an A grade
As a D is no good to me.

Aron Sopp (13)
St Guthlac's High School, Crowland

The Nan

What would I do without her?
She is warm, round and cuddly,
Her hair is silvery grey,
Her eyes are warm and sparkly,
What would I do without her?

What would I do without her?
She has always got time for me,
It's never too much to listen
I always get sympathy and tea,
What would I do without her?

What would I do without her?
She always gives me a cuddle
When I'm upset,
She always makes me laugh,
What would I do without her?

What would I do without her?
Her beds are nice and warm
For when we stay,
She always makes us feel welcome,
What would I do without her?

Aimee Hobbs (14)
St Guthlac's High School, Crowland

My Dad

This person is a lazy one,
He's always down the pub.
He's always in a temper
'Cause his son's always down the club.

There's not one peaceful moment,
When Dad's in a mood.
You argue and before you know it,
He's throwing a piece of food.

He's stronger than an ox,
Like all strong men he's dumb.
He likes heavy metal,
But it gives me a pain in the bum.

Always sleeping on the couch,
Rumbling like an earthquake.
No sound can wake him,
Except for the call of cake.

Really my dad is my hero,
He's also very protective.
If there's any problem, then
He's on it like a detective.

Liam Talbot (13)
St Guthlac's High School, Crowland

My Family

My dad Pat is a big pussycat,
He sleeps on the floor,
And snores with a roar.

My mum Chris is like a big sis,
We go out shopping until we are dropping.

My brother Glenn is like a big hen,
He flaps and flutters,
When my dad shouts and stutters,
'Glenn, give me that pen!'

My brother Shaun shows off on the lawn,
He sings and shouts and shuffles all about.

That's what my family's about.

Amy Breen (14)
St Guthlac's High School, Crowland

Lizards

Some lizards are big
Some lizards are small
Some like to dig
But some like to crawl
They sit in the sun
They like to hide in the trees
They all run around having fun
They like chewing on bumblebees
Some live in Spain
You can keep me as a pet
We're on the food chain
Don't take me to the vet.

Tony Cole (12)
St Guthlac's High School, Crowland

Friends

My friends are cool
We hang around the pool
We make biscuits in food
Everyone calls me cool

Tiffany is the best
Alex is a pest
Hilary is cruel!
We all shop at the mall

We all look fab!
We call a cab!
We go to school
And have to go to the hall.

We say goodbye
Then we hug and cry.

Lucy Hunt (13)
St Guthlac's High School, Crowland

My Sonnet

Computers are nice
My friends are the best
No matter the price
But I need a rest

I like to play football
I always run past
I think it is cool
My friends think I'm fast

I like cars that are cool
Others just drool
I like money
It's ever so funny

I like to go to the movies
They're just so groovy.

Matthew Venni (12)
St Guthlac's High School, Crowland

African Animals

Elephants thudding
Antelope leaping
Snakes slithering
Hippos swimming
Hyenas cackling
Monkeys swinging
But can't you have a laugh with a giraffe

Lions roaring
Cheetahs running
Leopards prowling
Tigers growling
Vultures soaring
Zebras drinking
But can't you have a laugh with a giraffe

Warthogs grunting
Flamingos dancing
Bats flapping
Koalas sleeping
Parrots squawking
Rhinos charging
But can't you have a laugh with a giraffe.

Nicholas Fletcher
St Guthlac's High School, Crowland

Young Writers - Away With Words Poems From Eastern England

Poem

Making a sonnet is very hard.
It took me nearly a whole hour
I done it on a piece of card . . .
Then I thought about a flower
I wanted something nice and pretty
I had a go and it was so bad
It was a little bit icy
All it was, was a little fad.
So I thought and thought again
Long and hard I thought all day
Oh it was a terrible pain
I couldn't think of anything to say
So I thought I'd write this poem
Just to tell you how it was going.

Amanda Hobbs (12)
St Guthlac's High School, Crowland

Firework's Night

On the 5th of November,
The sky is filled with light and we shout to the sky when my friends
come down to the ground, I think, *oh no, who's next?*

Finally it's my turn,
I feel a warm rod on my rope
I sizzle, sizzle, sizzle away
Why couldn't it be another day?
But as I say my prayers goodbye
I shoot up fast into the sky
I'm getting faster,
Oh no, I'm going to die . . .
Bang!
Now I'm just a light in the sky
As I float down I realise
I'm a firework and I'm going to die.

James Cobb (12)
St Guthlac's High School, Crowland

Chelsea FC

Blue is the colour
Chelsea is the name,
Blue is the colour
And Chelsea are the game.

They wave their flags so high
They nearly reach the sky,
They shoot, they score
And shout some more.

They are the best
They beat the rest.
Chelsea is the name!

Jordan Kirchin (13)
St Guthlac's High School, Crowland

My Mum And Dad

My mum is there every day,
And on Sundays too.
She makes sure my washing is done,
And my ironing too.
She does my lunch every morning,
And my dinner too.
She is there when I go to school,
And when I get home too.
She works all day and every day.
She is a very hard-working, busy mum,
She always takes care of me,
And is always there for me,
She is a great mum.

My dad is very helpful
And helps me do any work if I need his help.
So he gets a well-deserved rest sometimes at weekends.
He fixes things if they break,
To make them work again.
He works very hard during the week,
He is a great dad,
And a great DIY dad.

Elizabeth Thaddeus (12)
St Guthlac's High School, Crowland

Because

B e happy
E xcited,
C aring,
A nd
U seful
S o
E veryone is happy too.

Scott Howlett (12)
St Guthlac's High School, Crowland

Gawin

Gawin waits, for he hears the peasants come near,
He hears their footsteps come closer into the dark hills,
But the mighty dragon does not care, he does not fear,
All they think is he is here to kill and for their blood to spill
But all Gawin wants is to be free and live calm,
But instead he has been told to guard the hills,
But since the start the locals had seen him as harm,
They all think his aim is to kill
The great red dragon does not wish to harm,
Or roast them down to their bones,
But when the peasants see him they raise the alarm,
And cower in their small dark homes
And as the villagers come near
The mighty dragon dies with his one last fire tear.

Tom Johnstone (13)
St Guthlac's High School, Crowland

The Beach

The waves crash against the rocks
The sea air smells so sweet
All the girls in their pretty little frocks
And sitting on a beach front seat
You see the little boys playing on the rocks
Slipping and sliding on the mud
Now they've got dirty wet socks
The mums and dads tell them to be good
The ice cream van rings its bells
Every child jumps for joy
The ice cream man sells
Ice cream to all the girls and boys
The beach is nice, the beach is great
But to go to the beach is such a long wait.

Rebecca Thorpe (12)
St Guthlac's High School, Crowland

My Dog Spoty!

S poty is my dog's name!
P uppy eyes are so cute!
O n a walk he has fun!
T oys he plays with are so fun!
Y ou are the best dog ever!

Lauren Rostron (12)
St Guthlac's High School, Crowland

Football

On a wet and cold morning
Getting ready to play football
I'm already yawning
I feel like a snoozeball
Waiting for the whistle
We start so I pelt the ball
The ball goes down the ditch, I try to get it but I fall
I'm carried off the pitch
With a broken leg
Because I had fallen down the ditch
I felt dead
My mum and dad lay next to me in my hospital bed
Because all the time I just felt dead.

James Jones (12)
St Guthlac's High School, Crowland

The Funny Game Of Cricket

It should be played
On a summer's day
As the sun doesn't fade
Mostly probably in May
Hit this ball for six
On a perfect wicket
It'll get us out of a fix
That's just the ticket
If we win this game
This funny game of cricket
It will send us to fame
Just get that one last wicket
Here comes the rain
It's over once again.

Andrew Franklin (12)
St Guthlac's High School, Crowland

Class

I'm sitting here,
Next to this boy,
My best friend is near,
Using his pen as a toy.

I feel so cold,
But the sun's in my eye,
My teacher's not old,
And I'm about to cry.

I'm writing in my book,
Copying off a sheet,
Up and down I look,
Trying to keep it neat.

As soon as the bell goes,
Out the class flows!

Hilary Gloster (13)
St Guthlac's High School, Crowland

Homework Trouble!

As I woke up in the morning,
I had a look at my timetable,
My mum came up and gave me a homework warning,
As I stood up, I felt unstable.

As the bus pulled up outside my house,
I couldn't find my other shoe,
My dad said the cat caught a field mouse,
And I think my new bus driver is a Jew.

As I got to registration,
Thinking of an excuse for forgetting my homework,
I know! I left it at the train station,
As the teacher told me off, I couldn't help but smirk.

Now I have to stay in at break,
I'm thinking how long the homework will take.

Nathan Thorpe (13)
St Guthlac's High School, Crowland

Dreamer

Fast as the wind racing across the plain
With nostrils flaring and hooves pounding
Checking the boundaries of his domain
Other creatures leaping and bounding
None withstand him nor dare to defy
Masterful is he, so proud and so bold
Nothing can escape his watchful eye
His every move is a joy to behold
In the moonlight his coat softly glistens
Yet like a shadow he seems to pass
Then tossing his head he stops and listens
Silver and motionless upon the grass
But the darkness passes and the dawn will break
And my stallion vanishes as I awake.

Netanya Cassar (13)
St Guthlac's High School, Crowland

Why?

Girls who play football
Have to be tough
It can be gentle
It can be really rough

They can play football
With lots of skill
Which gives their spectators
Lots of thrill

Girls who play football
Get lots of stick
But oh my gosh
We can't half kick

We run all night, we run all day
But why the hell do we not get the pay?

Sam Woodham (13)
St Guthlac's High School, Crowland

My Animals

I have got a cute chocolate Labrador
She runs after sticks and answers to calls
She's big and fluffy and she's only four
She also loves chasing after her balls

I also have four beautiful kittens
They throw themselves at incoming adults
Especially when they wear bright mittens
They all stand way back if the big dog bolts

I have some chickens who nip and peck me
Delboy, the rooster, wakes us up at dawn
Sometimes at night they all hide in one tree
In a downfall of rain they look forlorn

Our house is a big farm as you can see
There is no other place I'd rather be!

Emma Smith (11)
St Guthlac's High School, Crowland

Sport!

Everybody loves sports,
Football, tennis, rugby, netball
Hundreds of sorts,
It's a hobby no one can resist!

When the sun comes out,
It's time to play,
The boys fish for trout,
Girls talk all day!

When the sun goes in,
Everyone turns around,
They pull up their quilts,
Without a sound.

In the morning they all awake,
For another good day of fun,
But if it rains, they cry, 'For God's sake!'
And carry on wishing for the sun.

Ryan Kirchin (11)
St Guthlac's High School, Crowland

If . . .

If boats sailed on the motorway
And tomato sauce was blue,
If football kits were made of silk
And tree trunks wore a shoe.

If motorbikes ran upwards
And milk floats really floated,
If beds were full of ugly pigs
And beans were sugar-coated.

If ants drove little cars
And eggs laid little chickens,
If we all had a tiger each
And monsters studied Dickens.

If babies' prams were motorised
And you listened to your conscience
If your brain was working properly
You wouldn't read this nonsense.

Hannah Stevens (11)
St Guthlac's High School, Crowland

Behind The Doors

Behind the doors
What lies inside?
A human beast?
A butterfly?
Behind the doors
What can it be?
The reflection of the moonlight sea?
Behind the doors
What noise inside?
A baby's laugh?
A kitten's cry?
Behind the doors
What's hidden there?
Who knows what secrets
Lurk and glare, behind the doors.

Lauren Marsters (11)
St Guthlac's High School, Crowland

The Necklace

The ring of diamonds around my neck
Seize my throat dry
Someone's pulling,
Someone's twisting,
I just wish I could know why.

It pinches my skin till blood runs cold,
Down past my neck.
I cannot breathe,
It won't stop with please,
This time it will make me a wreck.

I get pushed onto the garden wall,
While someone kicks my shins.
I fall to the ground,
Can't make any sound,
While dents are being made in my skin.

I was terrified about dying,
But now it seems so much worse.
This life will end,
It won't amend,
And this will be my last curse.

Rebecca Larter (12)
St Guthlac's High School, Crowland

School

Science
Dangerous experiments
Blue flames on Bunsen burners
Gas smells sour
Boiling water sounds like steam trains.

ICT
Computers blow out like fans
Keyboard and mice are hard like cheese
Silver screens with beautiful stands.

Design technology
Teacher shouts like strangers
Laughing like a funny clown
Taller than my dad
He is slim as a bin

Food technology
Chocolate is nice
Mixing our bowls as fast as we can
Cooking smells like food factories
Nice sweet chocolate like Cadbury

PE
Running like a leopard
Feet are sweating
Fast breathing like a sound of a dog.

Nicholas Wan (12)
St Guthlac's High School, Crowland

A Dream

As I lay down in bed,
And closed my eyes.
A noise in my head,
Gave me a surprise.

A girl dressed in blue,
Said to my face.
'Will you just shoo?'
And did up her lace.

The fish in the air,
Walking about.
One with blonde hair,
Was heading out.

So the dream that I had,
Was a bit mad.

Sarah Barber (12)
St Guthlac's High School, Crowland

The Rise Of The Sun

I once found a stranger alone in the world
And later that night I saw the angels twirl
She sang this by day and hummed it by night
Oh you should have seen her, it was a wonderful sight.

The blue sky turned lighter and lighter
As the sun began to rise
The blue sky turned brighter and brighter
As the sun increased in size

There were trees in the distance
As the sun began to rise
And houses non-existent
As the sun increased its size

The water flowing down the stream
As the sun began to rise
The trickle, trickle of the stream
As the sun increased its size

The blue sky turned dimmer and dimmer
As the sun began to set
The moon will be out
Tonight I bet.

Claire Alner-Brown (12)
St Guthlac's High School, Crowland

My Unfinished Poem

One day when it was quiet
I had nothing much to do
I took a pen and paper
And sat upon the loo

I'd been told to write a poem
A competition at my school
But thirty lines in total
Was the golden rule

As I sat there thinking
And chewing on my pen
There was shouting in the hallway
Was that my uncle Ken?

I jumped up from the toilet
And listened at the door
Why had he come around,
And what's he shouting for?

He'd come to take me shopping
For an early birthday gift
(I wanted something mobile
. . . if you get my drift)

We had to leave quite quickly
He didn't have much time
So I promptly flushed the toilet
And put aside this rhyme

We got badly stuck in traffic
And got back really late
So I had to leave the poem
Until another date

I never got it finished, but please don't shed a tear
I'm really not that bothered, I'll try again next year.

Mykal Hymas (12)
St Guthlac's High School, Crowland

Velvet Kisses

This is my precious rose
Whose romance is pure and sweet
In whom I love from my head to my toes
How this rose makes me complete
This rose is for someone special like a friend
For anytime day or night
A blooming, colourful, big bunch I'll send
This will surely make my friend feel bright
Morning sunrise, afternoon breeze, evening mist
This soft, beautiful rose has touched my heart
This rose has a scent, too many to list
From which I'll never depart
Oh how I will miss
This rose's glorious kiss.

Rebecca Candy (11)
St Guthlac's High School, Crowland

Countries

Cuba, China and England
Japan, Belgium and Finland
I'm writing about other places
Different origins, different faces

Brazil, Argentina, Chile and Peru
The Bahamas, Panama and Mexico too
Congo, Egypt, Mali and Chad
All these names are making me mad!

Tunisia, Angola, Libya, Sudan
Mongolia, India, Israel and Iran
Germany, Poland, Portugal, Spain
Latvia, Moldova, Sweden, Ukraine

I've told you of countries from Cuba - Ukraine
Now you can go back and read it again.

Jonjo Meade (11)
St Guthlac's High School, Crowland

Unwilted

My unwilted rose will never die,
This rose is the key to the light,
This rose makes my heart cry,
My rose equals my heart's delight,
This rose is better than a summer's day,
Thy precious rose is worth more to me than diamonds and gold.

Everlasting bright shining ray,
Stands strong in winter wet and cold,
Thy rose is sweeter than honey,
My rose is stronger than a tree,
Even cuter than a bumblebee,
Diamonds cover its eyes and nose,
For this is my unwilting rose.

Christina Rogers (11)
St Guthlac's High School, Crowland

Life Or Love?

Life is a mystery
Love is just a game
Life is birds ready to flee
Love is the thing between you and me
Life is the world
Love is just fate
Life is keeping us alive
Love is like honey in beehives
Children is life
You and I are love
So what is life?
And what is love?
They're both the same
They're both from above
This is the difference between life and love.

Rachel Rogers (11)
St Guthlac's High School, Crowland

Food

I love food
It puts me in a good mood
You have to have fruit
To help you shoot
To drop that ramp you must try
At least a bit of apple pie
And don't forget the yummy custard
And the spicy mustard
Chocolate cake is the best
And at Easter a chocolate nest
Ice cream is a lovely treat
And cheese tastes like your own feet
Chocolate muffins make you fat
Don't feed them to your cat
And remember cheese
Might make you sneeze
And never eat sheep
Because you will fall asleep
Zzzz.

James Smart (12)
St Guthlac's High School, Crowland

School Time!

When I get to school in the morning
I sit in the library nice and warm.
In the winter when the bell goes out
I go into the freezing cold snow
Into the glazing sun I go

It is Monday morning and first is PE
Off I go upstairs and get changed, no one watch me.

Next is RM, here I come
I will try not to hurt my thumb.

Then it is break I'll get some food
Probably a cookie, what would you choose?

Rebeccca Mackman (11)
St Guthlac's High School, Crowland

Mean Machine

It's blue and white
With silver handlebars
And skulls on the tyres
The seat is black
Just my size
My leather jacket matches my bike
My crash helmet matches too.
Gloves to keep control
Start slow
Open her up
Wind rushing
Acceleration
See the mud fly from the back tyre
Watch out!
Doughnut
Skim the wall
Into the hedge
Wheelie!
Speed freak
Got to slow down
Brake
Brake
Stop
My motorbike.

Clarke Chivers (11)
St Guthlac's High School, Crowland

I Compare Thee To A Rose

Shall I compare thee to a rose?
One that lasts on a summer's day
And in thy winter goes for a doze
And when blossoms come out in May
The colour of a romantic-red
The stem a grassy green
And thy as strong and thin as my lead
She of mine never turns mean
But thy rose grows never getting old
Thy wrinkles on thy delicate petals
No changes to soon turn cold
Thy will never die and be put in a coffin of metals
The eye will always be seen
For I, my love, will always be keen.

Bethany Mason (12)
St Guthlac's High School, Crowland

The Stinking Contest

Anyone heard about this stinking contest?
No it wasn't about who farts best.
The stinkiest skunk in the world was caught
And old 'Stinky' was to London brought.

The poor thing was put in a room in Big Ben,
And a challenge thrown open to all men.
Anyone who could stand for an hour Stinky's stink
Would win a supply of a whole year's drink.

The first contenders with stiff upper lips
Were outa there in moments with nasty quips,
Their cousins from across the sea remarked - 'Mon Dieu,
Of anyone winning this contest there is no fear.'

I could tell you about every failed contestant
But I'd be rambling on for days on end
So let's just skip on to the final bloke
Who happens to be the 'hero' of our joke.

In grand style arrived this big chap . . . a *blank*
I could tell you his race if I wanted to be frank
But just to give this joke a global factor
You fill the blank with your favourite racial character.

So into the room which like Hell stank
Walked in comfortably our dear *blank*.
Twenty minutes inside and not a sound.
We started thinking we had a winner found.

Thirty minutes and not a twitch,
'I think he's gonna win . . . the S.O.B'
As the clock, the 45 minute mark struck,
And people started talking of *blank's* pluck . . .

His surprise you can imagine, I have no doubt!
As ol' Stinky, (with his paw on his nose) ran out.

Tyla Lister (12)
St Guthlac's High School, Crowland

Daydream

As her eyes closed slowly
The breeze blew through her hair
She could hear the sea in the distance
And the children on the fair.

As she drifted off to sleep
The sun shone on her face
Her feet were buried in the sand.
Her hands just flopped like lace.

As she started dreaming
The raindrops started to fall
The first drop hit her on the nose
As she heard her husband call.

Come on love, hurry up!
You don't want to get wet
We'll go and get some fish 'n' chips
And dry off in the warm.

Then she realised where she was
Daydreaming after all.

Charley Sanders (12)
St Guthlac's High School, Crowland

Brothers

Some brothers are smart
Some brothers are dumb
While others can't do a simple sum
Some are unpredictable though some are not
Some are lazy, not do a lot
Most brothers are ugly, hardly any pretty
I don't know why we have them in this massive city
Most kids have brothers some not many, 1, 2, 3, maybe 4
Some lucky kids don't have any.
Why do we have them in this horrible place?
It feels like you're a prisoner
Like you're being punched in the face
Why are we cursed with them?
I just don't know
Oh brothers, oh brothers, oh brothers
When will you go?

Jodie Rainford (12)
St Guthlac's High School, Crowland

OCC

There is this show called American Chopper,
They build bikes even for coppers.
It is a family concern,
And if you watch it there is lots to learn.

Paul senior is the father,
His temper is enough to create a lather.
Mikey is the youngest son,
And by God he is somewhat dumb.

Of the firm Pauley is the brain,
His designs give the company fame.
Their bikes are known all over the states,
Their TV show earns them their million dollar rates.

Nicholas Geerlings (12)
St Guthlac's High School, Crowland

The Frightful Surprise

It was a dark and gloomy night.
You could not see the stars in the sky.
When I first heard that sound.
A blood-chilling cry.

I rushed from my bed to the window.
I looked out into the night.
And that is when I saw it.
It gave me such a fright.

There in the flower bed.
Were two green eyes.
Staring straight at me.
But that wasn't the biggest surprise.

The eyes started to move,
They were soon directly below.
And then in one big jump.
They were the other side of the window.

I jumped back and ran to the door.
It was locked - I started to scream.
I pounded my fists, I kicked my feet.
'Til I woke myself from my dream.

Catherine Fletcher (11)
St Guthlac's High School, Crowland

My Cat

I have a cat
Which sleeps on a mat

She caught a mouse
And brought it in my house

She eats a lot of food
When she's in a mood

Our settee is now torn
So now my mum's forlorn

My cat is nine and playful
But trust me she's a handful

She's not tall
But she's not small

As long as she's got a heartbeat
She will be lazing on a seat

She gives me a bite
But that's alright

She likes to take things
But she's not got my mum's rings

She pushes a ball
And can look like a fool.

Ben Smith (11)
St Guthlac's High School, Crowland

Grandpa's Ode To Golf

I take such graceful swings and watch the ball fly down the runway
And hope it don't land astray.
I wack the ball as hard as I can,
I hope I don't hit a gran
But then I'll get a ban so I better be scanning around.
Hole after hole I keep potting,
At least I'm in the final stretch
With only one hole left to play, what a good day!

Mitchell Capes (13)
St Guthlac's High School, Crowland

Football

F ootie, as 'they' say.

O nly played by the best.

O riginal.

T oo good for girls.

B est team ever (Man U!)

A lways on the telly.

L oved by all boys and men

L eeds, the worst team in the world.

Cian McCluskey (11)
St Guthlac's High School, Crowland

The Ocean

The ocean is for me and you
Oh so blue for me and you
So fresh and calm and windy too
Lots of fun for me and you

Starfish, catfish, shellfish
All sorts of fish in the big blue
All there for me and you

The ocean is for everyone
To see its delights under the sun
Big and small with all its wonders
A special place for me and you.

Leigh-Anne Casey (11)
St Guthlac's High School, Crowland

I Wonder

I wonder what it's like to be
In someone else's shoes.
Being someone who's not me,
The high times and the blues.
Watching the world through different eyes,
Listening through unknown ears.
Looking at the deep blue skies;
Quivering with fear.
Would my friends treat me the same
Or would they just walk past?
Would they even know my name?
I want to know . . . fast.
So I'm sitting here, writing this poem,
Wondering, thinking, still not knowing . . .

Sam Meade (13)
St Guthlac's High School, Crowland

Breaking A Horse

On this horse's back, he rears up high
Nostrils wide open and flaring.
Then belting fast to nearly fly.
Still sitting on his back, so scared but daring.
Hanging on for my dear life.
Round the trees he dares to wind
And the wind piercing my face like a knife
Look to his eye, fierce but kind
Before all this he had his pride
His movement innocent and unsure
For this horse could be a joy to ride
His feeling, somehow, needed me to explore
The way this horse now runs like lightning
And his manner was ever so frightening.

Stacey Arnold (12)
St Guthlac's High School, Crowland

Abandoned

Look at that cat
He really is sweet
Trying to catch a rat
He's looking for meat

He looks so thin
I think he's a stray
Eating from a tin
I really hope he'll be OK.

Shall I go help it
Call RSPCA
His green eyes are lit
Orange colour like hay.

I'm taking him home
So he won't be alone.

Abbie Youell (12)
St Guthlac's High School, Crowland

My Little Teddy Bear

I had a little teddy bear, its name was One-Eyed Jack.
I had a little teddy bear whose fur was brown and black.
I want another teddy bear who can be friends with me.
I would love another teddy bear and then we would be three.

Emily Attwood (13)
St Guthlac's High School, Crowland

I Like Snow

I like the snow
To make snowballs
It hurts I know

I like to make a snowman
You need eyes, nose and a mouth
I make big snowmen I can, I can

The snow is cold
Your hands freeze up
I played with my dad which is bold

The snow is white
It's made out of water
I play with my kite

Snow is soft
I throw it, *bang!* Hits Dad's head
Ha! Ha! I coughed

My mum comes out
Bang! Bang!
'Heads!' I shout

The snow is melting
My snowman is dead
Then the snow started belting

'Don't hit me with that snowball!'
Bang! Mum got hit again
Mum went in the hall

I like the snow
I wish it snowed all the time
I put my hair in a bow.

Vanessa Dorrian (11)
St Guthlac's High School, Crowland

Turning Back Time

I always think what it could be when you are in the old times.
The Victorians were evil, chopping heads off
And it is like tomato sauce coming out.
It was not nice!

We once were monkeys climbing trees, eating bananas.
We still do.
Starting to walk on two feet.
It was hard jumping from tree to tree.
Now no time is left.
We must go.
Going back to a home, that was fun.
But next time.
We take a look at the T-Rex!

Anton Van Marion (11)
St James' School, Grimsby

Turning Back Time

If only we could turn back time,
To speak to someone else's mind.
If only we could turn back time,
To the dreadful day of the accident.

If only we could turn back time,
To change Richard Hammond's mind,
To stop him sitting in the rocket car,
Hitting 288mph that caused an awful accident and near death.

If only we could turn back time,
To put bad things right.

Christy Mayo (12)
St James' School, Grimsby

Through The Eyes Of Mum

Mums have the hardest job going
They have a hard time looking after us
We don't give them anything back
They do everything for us
Some mums are horrible but my mum's so good to me
Mums are good to us
We need to give something back to them.

Chloe-Anne Reynolds (13)
St James' School, Grimsby

Turning Back In Time

I am whizzing back in time,
Whizzing, whizzing, whizzing,
Whizzing through everything,
The Earth, absolutely everything,
I am going quick, going slow,
Flying through the world I go,
All I see is Greenland,

And people waving goodbye,
I think I am going quicker, going slower,
And everything seems lower.

I feel smaller, oh no, I'm coming up to an object,
That's smaller than me,
Oh no, what could it be?
Some sort of mouse maybe!

Alex Benton (12)
St James' School, Grimsby

The Meaning Of Life

What is really the meaning of life?
My mum told me that her dad told her that leaving your life,
As a child is something you must do
But turning on people you love isn't the meaning of life
Money is *not* the meaning of life
Love, family, friends, that's the meaning of life
But you could have your own meaning of life
You can do what you want
Make your life worth living, use the time you have
Yes, do what you're told
But not if you can't
Especially if there's something you want to do
This is your life, you are in charge of your *life*
Soon after my grandad died
I never met my grandad, these words my mum spoke to me
I spoke back
I'm with my grandad and he's with me
My meaning of life is the way I want
What's yours?
Remember your life is yours not someone else's
After you read this I hope you read this, now!

Neil McCarthy (11)
St James' School, Grimsby

Through The Eyes Of A Hobo

What is my purpose?
What is my meaning?
Maybe I am an amusement.
Or a joke to society?
Why am I alive?
What should I do?
Why won't I die? God damn you,
People laugh and joke,
They throw food at me with bottles of Coke.
Do you hate me? Yes you do.
Now years have gone,
I am sick, throwing up,
About to die, thank you.

Dean Parkinson (12)
St James' School, Grimsby

The Meaning Of Life

What really is the meaning of life?
Does anyone really know?
We could all have a guess,
But which is really true?
You could try to be someone else,
But that wouldn't be you.
So we could all have a go,
But why? You could just be yourself,
Come on now,
Let's have some fun,
Run, run, run and swim, swim, swim.
Down a slide of ice,
Splash in a bowl of sauce,
Thick and gloopy,
I guess that is a meaning of life,
What's yours? 'Cause that's mine.
Or is it the same?

Rebecca Procter (13)
St James' School, Grimsby

Through The Eyes Of The Mirror

Truth always told.
No secrets on hold
Your hair intact
I speak only fact
I reflect on all
It is easy to recall
Seen many a dance
Many people prance
I have no trouble
In creating double
No lies, everything real
Then the world might just heal.

Alice Cleve (13)
St James' School, Grimsby

Through The Eyes Of An Actor

Waiting for work with nothing to do,
Who would have chosen this profession,
Would you?
Battling it out for a part you adore,
Only to find the producer thinks you're a bore!
On the telly it looks so easy,
But now I'm centre stage I feel queasy.

Eleanor Thompson (12)
St James' School, Grimsby

Through The Eyes Of A Chocolate Cake

Through the eyes of a chocolate cake,
You'd see yourself rise and bake.
Out of the oven you would come,
Heated but rather glum.

Left there to cool,
In a chocolate kind of pool.
Put in a fridge for a while,
Till you are a hard chocolate pile.

Covered in icing
Before you need slicing.
Topped with cherries,
And a few other berries.

Here comes the knife, sharp and long,
And out comes your chocolatey pong.
There's the mouth open wide,
It looks like you'll be going inside.

Crisp and crunchy, tasty too,
Your chocolate melts like splodgy glue.
You went down such a hit,
That everyone ate every last bit.

So would you like to be a chocolate cake,
Waiting in that oven ready to bake?
Let's be glad you're not a cake,
Waiting patiently to bake.

Amelia Carroll (13)
St James' School, Grimsby

Life . . . Interest?

Life is very interesting,
People used to be very intelligent,
But . . . is the Devil?
He makes everyone follow him,
To be disobedient to our lovely Father,
To do everything opposite,
People will say a lot of naughty words, and do naughty things.
Our parents will make us follow the right way,
Our life goes day by day.
Life is wonderful,
We can make ourselves be good,
It is very interesting.

Kevin Ho (13)
St James' School, Grimsby

Through The Eyes Of A Scientist

What science means to me.
Is all make believe you see.

Is not what children learn at school
You don't have to go by the rules.

If guns weren't invented there would be no wars.
But people couldn't climb up walls.

Science is a lot you see.
Does it mean the same to you - as to me?

Laura Forster (12)
St James' School, Grimsby

Time

If only we could turn back time,
To see Shakespeare and rhyme.
If only we could turn back time,
To stop the Twin Towers from burning down.
If only, if only we could turn back time,
I definitely would not die.
If we all turned back time
We could see the prehistoric land of time.

Ella Blanchard (11)
St James' School, Grimsby

The Meaning Of Life

The meaning of life
What is the meaning of life?
Is life just about fun and games
Or is it about hard work?
What do you think?
Well, I think the meaning of life is to do the right things!
To have a life of peace
A life where there's no fighting, bullying and racism
A life where no bad things will happen
A life you would love to live again, full of happiness and love
Not hatred and destruction
That is what I think the meaning of life is
    What are your thoughts?

Evans Mauta (11)
St James' School, Grimsby

Tinkerbell

Fly away, fly away from all your mistakes,
Your broken promises and your heartbreaks,
Try, try your hardest to believe you don't care
You don't love and you won't share.
Silence yourself, to deafen the demons,
To tell your fantasy and live the dream,
Because the more you run,
The less breath you have,
So kick away the floor and sway in the draft,
Sway until you fly at last.

Rachel De Saint Pern (14)
Summerhill School, Leiston

Young Writers Information

We hope you have enjoyed reading this book - and that you will continue to enjoy it in the coming years.

If you like reading and writing poetry drop us a line, or give us a call, and we'll send you a free information pack.

Alternatively if you would like to order further copies of this book or any of our other titles, then please give us a call or log onto our website at www.youngwriters.co.uk

Young Writers Information
Remus House
Coltsfoot Drive
Peterborough
PE2 9JX

(01733) 890066